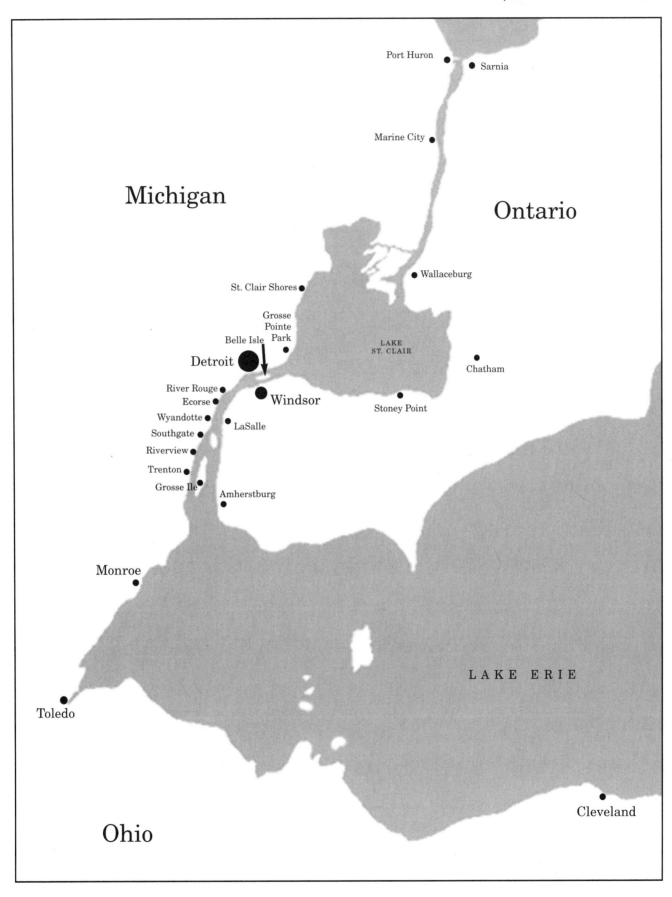

Port Huron
Sarnia

Marine City

Michigan

Ontario

Wallaceburg

St. Clair Shores

Grosse
Pointe
Park

Belle Isle

LAKE
ST. CLAIR

Detroit

Chatham

River Rouge
Ecorse

Windsor

Stoney Point

Wyandotte
LaSalle

Southgate

Riverview

Trenton

Grosse Ile

Amherstburg

Monroe

LAKE ERIE

Toledo

Ohio

Cleveland

Rum Running

AND THE

Roaring Twenties

An aerial view of the Detroit River in 1925 demonstrates graphically one of the main avenues of rumrunners. Belle Isle is seen in the distance. Courtesy: Burton Historical Collection.

Rum Running

AND THE

Roaring Twenties

*Prohibition on the
Michigan-Ontario Waterway*

PHILIP P. MASON

 Wayne State University Press   Detroit

GREAT LAKES BOOKS

A complete listing of the books in this series
can be found at the back of this volume.

Endpaper maps prepared by Marshall Henrichs,

based on a detailed map by Leo Kuschel.

Library of Congress Cataloging-in-Publication Data

Mason, Philip P. (Philip Parker), 1927-
     Rumrunning and the roaring twenties: prohibition on the Michigan-
Ontario Waterway / Philip P. Mason
          p.   cm. — (Great Lakes books)
     Includes bibliographical references (p.) and index.
     ISBN 0–8143–2583–1 (alk. paper)
     1. Prohibition—Michigan—Detroit—History—20th century. 2. Smug-
gling—Detroit River (Mich. and Ont.)—History—20th century. 3.Smuggling—
Michigan—Detroit—History—20th century. 4. Smuggling—Ontario—Windsor—
History—20th century. 5. Prohibition—United States—History—20th century.
6. Detroit (Mich.)—History—20th century. 7. Windsor (Ont.)—History—20th century. I. Title. II. Series.
HV5090.M5M37 1995
364. 13′3—dc20
                                                             95-4610

CONTENTS

PREFACE

THE PASSAGE of the Prohibition Amendment to the Michigan Constitution in 1916 and its subsequent counterpart—the Eighteenth Amendment to the United States Constitution in 1918—ushered in an exciting chapter in the history of the Michigan–Ontario region and especially those communities along the Detroit River. For the fifteen years in which the manufacture, sale, and consumption of alcoholic beverages was illegal, citizens of Detroit and surrounding communities on both sides of the border engaged in pervasive violation of the Volstead Act and state and local laws. Thousands of Michigan citizens were arrested and convicted, but they represented only a small segment of the number involved in these illegal activities. Many more who frequented blind pigs and speakeasies also violated the law, but they were rarely apprehended by police. The stories, statistics, and pictures provide captivating and staggering material for those interested in this dramatic era.

This book is not intended to be a definitive history of Prohibition in the United States or in Michigan and Ontario. Such studies have already been written, based upon careful research. The most notable and comprehensive studies on the Michigan scene have been written by Larry Engelmann, whose book *Intemperance: The Lost War Against Liquor* and numerous articles have covered the Prohibition years in detail. This study attempts rather to fill a gap in the existing published accounts with a selection of photographs, cartoons, and other illustrations that demonstrate dramatically how the campaign for Prohibition was waged. It will illustrate visually the various innovative techniques used to smuggle liquor into Michigan from Canada, the illicit operations of commercial and home stills, the patrons of speakeasies and blind pigs, and the successful and failed efforts at enforcing the Volstead Act.

Visual sources have often been overlooked in the published studies of the period. Instead, writers have relied almost totally upon the written archival sources, newspapers, journals, and police files. This study will demonstrate vividly the significance and unique contribution of photographs and cartoons as historical records—just as significant as the contemporary accounts written during Prohibition. Each of the five chapters of visual images in this study is introduced by a brief written account, highlighting the events of the chapter's focus.

During the preparation of this book I was in contact with hundreds of persons who had something special to tell me about Prohibition. Some were actually involved in rumrunning across the Detroit River and Lake St. Clair. Others operated blind pigs and speakeasies. In fact, so many sources told me of the stills they operated, that it is a wonder smuggled liquor from Canada was needed. In addition to first-hand accounts, others have described similar activities of their parents, relatives, and friends. Despite all the illegal activities involved, there has been little, if any, hesitation in relating these accounts. In fact, the informants seem to take great pride in describing the activities of the rumrunners and others they knew who were involved in violating the law. The rumrunning accounts are now as appealing as the rumrunning activities were in the 1920s.

ACKNOWLEDGMENTS

MANY INSTITUTIONS and individuals have participated in the preparation of this book. The research for the narrative account of Prohibition involved use of the rich archival resources at the Burton Historical Collection of the Detroit Public Library, the Bentley Library at the University of Michigan, the Michigan State Archives, the Toronto Provincial Archives, and the historical archives and local historical societies in the metropolitan Detroit area. The records of the U.S. District Court and the files of Detroit, Port Huron, Windsor, Toledo, and Cleveland newspapers also contained valuable information about rumrunners, speakeasies, stills, gangs, and others who violated the Volstead Act on a massive scale.

A far more difficult task was locating suitable photographs, cartoons, and other illustrations, especially those that had not been used before in publications. I wish to give special thanks to Noel Van Gorden, John Gibson, and David Poremba of the Burton Historical Collections; John Curry, photographic archivist at the Michigan State Archives; and Corrado Santoro and Stormie Stewart of the Ontario Public Archives. Jeannette Bartz of the *Detroit News* and Denise Chuk of the *Windsor Star* graciously shared their outstanding Prohibition photograph collections. C. H. (Marty) Gervais, whose book, *The Rumrunners: A Prohibition Scrapbook,* was an invaluable resource, made available his fine collection of Windsor photographs. Maureen Mullin of the Cleveland Public Library was also helpful in locating key photographs in their remarkable audio–visual collection. As always, I received assistance from Margery Long, audio–visual curator at the Archives of Labor and Urban Affairs at Wayne State University.

Acknowledgments

Special thanks is due to Deborah Kingery of the Wayne State University Media Services, who copied many of the photographs needed in the book. Peter Blum, archivist for the Stroh Brewery, located a number of excellent photographs and illustrations relating to that company's activities during Prohibition.

Several individuals made available their personal photograph collection. Gene Buel of Marine City, Michigan, provided several excellent photographs of Prohibition scenes on the St. Clair River. Florence Ledyard allowed me to copy from the Livingstone–Odell–Ledyard Collection in the Burton Historical Collection a Detroit Club meeting announcement commemorating the end of the era of John Barleycorn in Detroit. From Nell Rhoades I obtained the delightful photographs showing her in the 1930s posing with devices used to smuggle liquor into Detroit.

I am especially indebted to my longtime colleagues and friends, Jo Ellen Vinyard of Eastern Michigan University and Larry Kulisek of the University of Windsor, for reading the manuscript drafts of the book and making suggestions to improve it. John Polasek, director of the Dossin Great Lakes Museum, and Cynthia Bieniek, who assisted him in the preparation of the Prohibition exhibit at the museum, were helpful in a variety of ways, especially in sharing photographs and research materials. Roger Rosenstreter, editor of *Michigan History* magazine, and Carey L. Draeger, assistant editor, gave special attention to the article, "If You Couldn't Get a Drink You Weren't Trying," which appeared in the September/October 1994 issue. Detroit historian Arthur Woodford has supported the project from its inception two years ago and has shared his research and views on issues relating to Prohibition in Detroit. Lorraine Brown, guest curator of the Seagrams Museum, has also been of assistance in explaining Canadian liquor regulations during Prohibition. Marsha Haines of Port Huron and her colleague Jill Carson, feature writer on the *Port Huron Times Herald*, gave me valuable information about rumrunning and the operation of illegal stills along the St. Clair River. Ron Voelker shared with me his research on the Prohibition era in the Detroit and surrounding communities.

A number of individuals have given me firsthand accounts of their experiences during Prohibition and tales from their parents and relatives. My friend Leonard Simons told me of his exciting experience with members of the Purple Gang. Sally Spitzley and Florence Ledyard gave interesting anecdotes about their experiences as young children during Prohibition.

The main sponsor of the Prohibition exhibit at the Dossin Great Lakes Museum has been the Great Lakes Maritime Institute under the leadership of Malcolm McAdam, its president. It was his idea for this volume, and he has supported it in many ways but especially in locating relevant materials and reviewing the manuscript. Two other board members of the

Institute have been especially helpful. The distinguished maritime artist Leo Kuschel prepared a detailed map of the Detroit River and Lake St. Clair for use as an endpaper. Paul Moehring copied many photographs and cartoons for use in the book. The active support from Maud Margaret Lyon, the director of the Detroit Historical Museum, has been indispensable.

The staff of the Wayne State University Press supported the project in all phases. I am especially indebted to Barbara Muzzin, who assisted in the preparation of the captions, and to Alice Nigoghosian and Arthur Evans, and especially to Kathryn Wildfong, the managing editor of the Press, who in her own competent professional way coordinated the production of the book through its various stages.

Marshall Henrichs, the designer, deserves special thanks for his imaginative layout of the illustrations and the jacket.

Catherine Phillips provided invaluable help in her research on Prohibition, which she shared with me. And, finally, I thank Marcia Heringa Mason for supporting and encouraging me through every stage of preparation for the book, for assisting me in the research and photograph selections, for typing and editing the various drafts of the manuscript, and for sharing my enthusiasm and interest in this fascinating era.

To all those mentioned, as well as others whose help and encouragement is less easy to pinpoint, my heartfelt appreciation.

CHAPTER

1

MICHIGAN'S PROHIBITION EXPERIMENT

SPRING TRAINING

I N THE SPRING OF 1919 WHEN the legislature of the state of Michigan ratified the Eighteenth Amendment to the United States Constitution—a measure prohibiting the manufacture, sale, and consumption of alcoholic beverages—it marked nearly a century of active campaigning for Prohibition in Michigan. As early as 1852 the Michigan state legislature had taken action to forbid the manufacture or sale of alcoholic drinks, and although the state supreme court later declared the law unconstitutional, the campaign for Prohibition continued unabated. By 1911 forty of Michigan's eighty–three counties had adopted "dry" ordinances.[1]

After the turn of the twentieth century, the Prohibition movement gathered momen-

tum throughout the United States and especially in Michigan. On November 7, 1916, following a carefully conceived and orchestrated campaign against saloons, breweries, and distilleries, the voters of Michigan approved an amendment to the state constitution prohibiting the sale of liquor, beer, and wine by a vote of 353,373 to 284,754. The amendment was to take effect on May 1, 1918, making Detroit the first city of the United States with a population in excess of 250,000 to go dry.[2]

The success of Prohibitionists in Michigan resulted from a variety of factors. Under the active direction of the Michigan Anti–Saloon League, founded in 1893, and a coalition of church, business, and community leaders, a well–organized campaign was mounted throughout the state, not only in rural areas where

13

Prohibition sentiment was already strong, but also in Detroit, Flint, Saginaw, Grand Rapids, and other populated centers where there had traditionally been strong opposition to any curbs upon the use of alcoholic beverages.

Michigan business leaders took an active role on behalf of Prohibition. They supported the view that the widespread use of beer and liquor by workers sharply reduced productivity and increased absenteeism. Henry Ford took the issue a step farther than just preaching the cause of Prohibition. Within the Ford Motor Company he established a special, well–staffed sociological department to monitor the behavior of workers and their families and to curb the use of alcohol. Ford staff members were sent to the homes of workers to evaluate their lifestyles and personal habits. Thrift and frugality were encouraged and rewarded, and the rental of rooms to boarders was discouraged in order to promote stronger family ties. Those workers who failed to meet Henry Ford's rigid moral standards could not qualify for the company's coveted five–dollar–a–day wage. Excessive use of liquor resulting in drunkenness was cause for immediate dismissal. Although other business leaders disagreed with Ford's views on the evils of alcohol or with his paternalism, they supported Prohibition in order to improve worker productivity.[3]

Michigan church leaders, long active in the temperance movement, also took a leading role in the campaign for a state Prohibition amendment. They used the pulpit and church facilities to organize community groups and influence public attitude toward drinking. In a brilliant public relations coup they brought into Michigan the charismatic and nationally known revivalist and evangelist, William "Billy" Sunday, for a series of sermons, lectures, and public appearances.[4] A former big league baseball player for the Chicago White Stockings and an ordained minister, Billy Sunday had attracted a national following for his stand on drinking.

During the months before election in the fall of 1916, Billy Sunday visited most of the urban areas of Michigan, giving his famous "Booze Sermon," more sedately called "Get on the Water Wagon."[5] In a style later perfected by a modern generation of evangelists he whipped up the audiences into a frenzy, darting across the stage, jumping on chairs and tables, and flailing his arms to make a point about the evils of alcohol. "Liquor," he railed, "is the blood sucker of humanity; it is God's worst enemy and hell's best friend."[6] He gave vivid descriptions of the excesses of drinking—the breakup of families, the plight of homeless children and orphans, prostitution, crime, and finally a sickness that leads to death. "When I go to the ring with John Barleycorn," he challenged, "they will find me on my feet, my wind good, and ready to go to the limit."[7]

Tens of thousands of Michigan citizens

turned out to hear the popular reformer in churches, schools, public arenas, and private homes. He stopped at the gates of Detroit, Flint, and Saginaw automobile factories and urged workers to stop drinking and join the Prohibition campaign. In 1916 he met with three hundred of Detroit's most prominent social and community leaders at the home of John S. Newberry in Grosse Pointe and asked for their support. While in Detroit he was always a guest of S. S. Kresge, the nationally known business magnate.[8] University students were also targeted by the Reverend Sunday. At the University of Michigan in 1916 he enlisted a thousand students to work in the forthcoming election on behalf of the Prohibition amendment. "I will fight them till hell freezes over," he told the students, "then I'll buy a pair of skates and fight 'em on the ice."[9]

Billy Sunday and other Prohibitionists aimed their main attacks on saloon keepers, distillers, and brewers. "They were no less than the hand maidens of hell," Sunday railed.[10] German brewers were the special target of his invective. "They turn our idea of the Sabbath into the continental idea with their beer gardens and beer drinking."[11] Another related theme of Sunday's attacks was his claim that the foreign born were responsible for crime and the horrible drinking problems of the nation.

Reformers within the political arena also constantly cited the corrupt power of brewers, distillers, and saloon operators. They predicted that the passage of the Prohibition Amendment would end the stronghold of the liquor lobby and bring a return to honest government in Michigan.

The Allied war effort also found its way into the campaign. Prohibition leaders argued that hundreds of thousands of bushels of grain should be used for foodstuffs for Allied soldiers and civilians and not for booze. German brewers and distillers in Detroit and other Michigan communities soon found themselves the target of reformers who characterized them as the "enemies of temperance and enemies of peace."[12]

The decisive victory of state Prohibition in the November 1916 election—even in the traditionally "wet" urban centers—was a tribute to the leadership of reformers and the distinctive role of Billy Sunday who crystallized public opinion about the abuses and evils of alcohol and its role in compromising the Allied war effort. In the weeks that followed the November election, the state legislature passed several measures to implement the Prohibition Amendment. The Damon Law prohibited the bringing in of liquor from other states and foreign countries. The enforcement of Prohibition was assigned to the State Constabulary (Michigan State Police) and the Michigan Food and Drug Commission.[13]

The passage of the amendment in

November 1916 did not end immediately the manufacture, sale, or consumption of alcoholic beverages in Michigan. That date was set for May 1, 1917. This six–month delay enabled the owners of restaurants, hotels, taverns, saloons, and private clubs, as well as private citizens, to stockpile huge quantities of beer, wine, and hard liquor. In the weeks before the deadline, liquor stores, saloons, and taverns did a whirlwind business waiting until the final hours to close.

The prestigious Detroit Club held a special meeting to call attention to the May deadline. On April 20, 1917, it invited all members to a banquet "to attend the obituary of John Barleycorn." The dinner featured "one Beefsteak Dinner garnished with rare condiments and spices, steeped in nectar, and fragrant as the attar of the festive onion." The announcement of the meeting further called attention to the upcoming event. "The obsequies Being the Vale ere thou steppeth on that aqueous chariot, known as the 'Water Wagon' which will sway from the 'Milky Way' at 12:01 a.m., May the first. No ladies invited."[14]

Within hours after the May curfew began, a smuggling network was established from the state of Ohio, and especially Toledo, a mere sixty miles from metropolitan Detroit and connected by the heavily traveled Dixie Highway. Monroe, Michigan, located between the two urban centers, became the mecca for bootleggers who congregated there to oversee their smuggling operations. To a lesser degree the Detroit River became a route used to bring contraband liquor into Detroit and other Michigan cities located along the Michigan–Ontario waterway.[15]

Smugglers creatively utilized a variety of methods to bring liquor, wine, and beer across the Ohio border into Michigan and past the local police officers. Some individuals traveled to and from Toledo by interurban, railroad, and bus carrying shopping bags and suitcases filled with liquor. One Detroit woman, who was observed often traveling to Toledo to "visit a sick relative," was finally apprehended by a suspicious police officer. When examined by a matron, they discovered "twelve hot water bottles filled with rye whiskey hung around her person from an ingeniously contrived belt."[16]

In the months that followed other clever devices were discovered by alert police officers. Rubber belts, false breasts, chest protectors similar to those worn by baseball catchers and umpires, loaves of bread hollowed out to hold bottles of whiskey, and suitcases with false compartments were put into use as vessels of the forbidden liquid by passengers on buses and trains.

Different techniques were employed by those who had automobiles and trucks. Many took their children with them as decoys on rumrunning trips, giving the impression of a family outing. If stopped by authorities, the children were primed to shout, cry, or create confusion and thereby discourage careful automobile searches.

More sophisticated and ingenious methods were tried out and perfected. Smugglers rebuilt automobiles to provide hidden compartments under the seat, roof, or trunk. The gas tanks on a fleet of twenty–five Ford automobiles were removed and replaced by ones with two separate compartments—one for fuel, the other for whiskey. Trucks were also altered to provide hidden space under the floor boards for cases of liquor. Indeed, many of these ingenious techniques to hide contraband liquor later inspired smugglers during national Prohibition to utilize and even perfect the methods.

The state legislature of Michigan assigned the task of enforcing Prohibition measures to the Michigan Food and Drug Commission and to the Michigan State Police under the command of Colonel Roy C. Vandercook. With the cooperation and assistance of local police agencies, the officers boarded buses, interurbans, and railroad trains to check passengers. In addition, they also stopped suspicious looking automobiles and trucks for inspection and installed sentry boxes at strategic locations along the Dixie Highway in order to monitor traffic.

Smugglers recognized immediately the danger of police inspection and devised schemes to avoid detection and arrest. They used circuitous routes to avoid police road blocks, they drove at night and on holidays, and they traveled in caravans for protection against hijackers, as well as police. They often tried to run police blockades. The Michigan State Police, in response to the tactics of smugglers, counteracted with their own methods to apprehend criminals. Undercover police officers kept Toledo liquor stores and suspected liquor warehouses under surveillance. They paid informers to provide information on the date, time, and extent of shipments.

In the spring of 1919 state police introduced a more imaginative scheme to apprehend smugglers. At a strategic location along the Dixie Highway, by now called the "Avenue de Booze," two squads of police were stationed one hundred yards apart. When smugglers refused to stop for inspection at the first station, the northernmost squad, upon signal, dropped a huge telephone pole across the highway. An incident in March 1919 ended predictably. A smuggler traveling seventy miles an hour hit the barrier and bounded thirty feet into the air, projecting the car's occupants and dozens of bottles of whiskey onto the pavement. However, despite the effectiveness of this system, there was immediate public outcry against it, and Colonel Vandercook reported that "higher ups seemed to think it a bit informal, so we abandoned it."[17]

The Ohio–Michigan smuggling operation attracted more than just the amateur smuggler. Organized gangs took part in the action as well. In fact, the opportunities for huge profits brought criminals from other parts of the country to Michigan. The most notorious were the Billingsley brothers—Logan, Ora, and Sherman. They arrived in Detroit within a few weeks after the November 1916 election—already with criminal records in Oklahoma, Washington, and West Virginia. They rented a warehouse in Toledo and stocked it with thousands of bottles of liquor. In Detroit they opened a grocery store and garage on Trumbull Avenue. Their business flourished, especially after May 1917 when state Prohibition went into effect. They sold beer and whiskey to trusted customers and they provided a delivery service to about thirty-five Detroit hotels and restaurants. Their profits were substantial. A case of whiskey costing eight to ten dollars in Toledo sold for seventy–five dollars in Detroit.

The Billingsley smuggling enterprise ended in September 1918 when the brothers were arrested near Monroe. Tipped off by an informer, the state police seized a caravan of automobiles with a cargo of 1,500 quarts of high–grade whiskey, valued at $12,000 to $15,000.[18]

In a trial held in January 1919 in the U.S. District Court in Detroit, Judge Arthur Tuttle convicted Sherman and Ora Billingsley of violating the smuggling pro-visions of the Webb– Kenyon Law (Logan was then serving a sentence in a federal penitentiary for bringing liquor into the state of Washington), noting that the Billingsley family had consistently defied the liquor laws in the United States with a total of forty–eight arrests. Judge Tuttle admonished the brothers with the statement: "You fellows have got it into your heads . . . that it was smart to defy the laws and you thought you could get away with it here [in Detroit]."[19] Judge Tuttle sentenced them to two years and six months in Leavenworth Prison. Although the Billingsley brothers were not the only gang convicted in Michigan, they were perhaps the best known in the early years of Prohibition in Michigan.

Records are not available to tally the total amount of liquor smuggled into Michigan between May 10, 1917, and May 24, 1919, when Prohibition went into effect in Ohio. The amount was substantial. According to Frederick Woodworth, the head of the Michigan Food and Drug Commission, more than 800,000 quarts of whiskey were seized by police between May 10, 1917, and February 1918, mostly along the Dixie Highway.[20] Indeed, so much contraband liquor was seized in Monroe County alone that there were no storage facilities. Many of the 60,000 gallons confiscated were placed in the home of the sheriff of Monroe. The liquor not subsequently destroyed was sent to Grand Rapids where it was converted to automobile anti–freeze.[21]

Police arrests of smugglers for violation of the state's Damon Law prohibiting the bringing in of liquor to Michigan provide widespread evidence of illegal rum-running. During the first month of Prohibition nearly a thousand citizens were arrested and convicted for smuggling. The jail in Monroe, designed to hold a maximum of twelve prisoners, was usually packed daily with forty or so offenders from whom an average of sixteen quarts of whiskey each had been confiscated. In fact, so many smugglers were apprehended in Monroe County that the local circuit court had to hold continuous sessions to handle the caseload.[22]

The fear of arrest and conviction for smuggling obviously did not deter the criminal activity, except for those who might be embarrassed by the negative publicity; nor did the penalties. The first offense for smuggling carried a fine of about $20. According to Commissioner Woodworth, an estimated 90 percent of those convicted paid their fines and "went away whistling."[23] The Wayne County courts were so lenient that many smugglers got off without even a fine. Commissioner Woodworth proposed a solution for improving the ineffective local judicial situation and for putting a stop to smuggling: "If we could get one of our up–state judges down in Wayne County, we could break it up in a month."[24]

The leniency of Michigan laws and judges was, of course, not the only factor in the widespread incidence of smuggling liquor into Michigan between 1917 and 1919. The huge profits realized from the sale of contraband booze attracted thousands into the smuggling occupation. During most of the two–year Ohio "wet" period, a quart of whiskey which cost from $2.00 to $2.50 in Toledo sold for from $8.00 to $15.00 in Detroit and other Michigan cities. As the private supplies of beer, wine, and whiskey dried up in the summer of 1918, the prices for illegal booze rose even more sharply, reflecting the market conditions. The common practice of diluting whiskey in speakeasies and blind pigs provided even greater profits. Commissioner Woodworth gave further evidence of the tremendous profits from smuggling in March 1919 when he reported that the 800,000 quarts of contraband liquor seized by Michigan authorities, which cost about $1.6 million in Ohio, would have fetched $8 million in Detroit.[25]

The enforcement of Michigan's Prohibition laws received a major setback in 1919 during a controversial legal case involving August Marxhausen, a leader of Detroit's influential German community, the editor of *Abend Post*, and incidentally an outspoken critic of Prohibition. In August 1918, acting on a warrant by Wayne County's prosecuting attorney, the Michigan State Police raided the Marxhausen estate on Calf Island near Grosse Ile. Six thousand bottles of beer were confiscated along with a portrait of Otto Von

Bismarck, and Marxhausen was arrested and convicted of "illegal possession of liquor."[26] Enraged, Marxhausen appealed and on February 18, 1919, the Michigan Supreme Court issued its decision to rule against the state. The court ruled that the police did not have a proper search warrant and that Marxhausen could not be arrested for merely having liquor in his home. The court also ruled the Damon Law unconstitutional and thus prohibited the state from prosecuting individuals for the bringing in or possessing of liquor.[27]

The impact of the state supreme court decision was felt within hours. On February 19, Marxhausen's beer, minus seven hundred bottles which had disappeared, was returned to his home. State and local police officials issued orders to stop arrests for smuggling, and judges freed prisoners from jails. Even confiscated liquor was returned to the prisoners. Thousands of automobiles jammed the highways to Toledo in what local newspapers described as "the Great Booze Rush."[28] Two months later the action of the Ohio legislature accomplished what the Michigan State Police could not. By prohibiting the manufacture and sale of liquor in Ohio it dried up the source of Michigan's smugglers.

Michigan's two–year experiment in Prohibition provided an interesting, even exciting, chapter in its history. There was excitement and glamour in the exploits of smugglers, and speakeasies and blind pigs opened in large number in Detroit and other Michigan cities. But the lessons learned about Prohibition from the "Ohio–Michigan Connection"—as it was described by one authority—were mixed. It was a boon to both the individuals and organized gangs involved, who not only made huge profits from bootlegging but also mastered sophisticated techniques of smuggling contraband liquor, operating illegal stills, and running speakeasies and blind pigs. Within a year, when the Eighteenth Amendment went into effect, they became the cadre of smugglers who for the thirteen years of national Prohibition made astronomical profits and at the same time defeated the concerted efforts of national, state, and local law enforcement officials to enforce the Volstead Act.

The Prohibition experiment made police agencies aware of the major task of enforcing laws unpopular to groups from all walks of life. They learned firsthand of the imaginative techniques and devices employed to smuggle liquor and to operate blind pigs and speakeasies. The blatant bribery of police officials was another lesson learned by the Ohio–Michigan episode.

"Spring Training" was over in 1919, and the regular season began a year later.

Fillmore's Prohibition Songs was popular among Prohibition reformers and used extensively at rallies and public meetings. Cincinnati: Fillmore Music House, 1900.

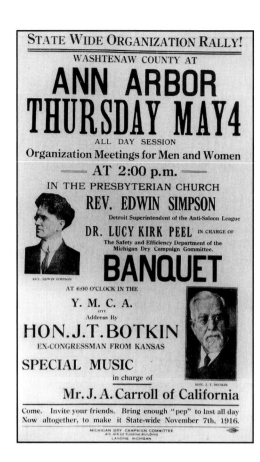

The Michigan Dry Campaign Committee sponsored this meeting in Ann Arbor, May 4, 1916. Courtesy: Bentley Library, University of Michigan.

March of the Women's Christian Temperance Union, Ann Arbor, 1909. Courtesy: Michigan State Archives.

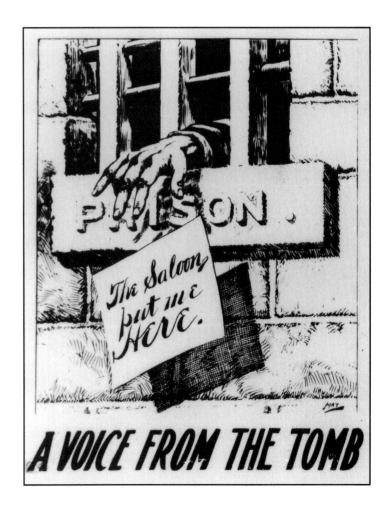

For more than two decades the Anti–Saloon League led the campaign for statewide Prohibition in Michigan. Courtesy: Michigan State Archives.

The father's hard–earned wages are swallowed up in whiskey.

Cartoonists played a key role in the temperance and Prohibition movements. One of the popular arguments depicted in the cartoons was the "evil" influence of liquor and the tavern in breaking up the family. Courtesy: Bentley Library, University of Michigan.

Enter the starving daughter, dressed in rags and scorned by friends.

He forms a resolution and leaves the tavern.

Returning home, he gives his wages to wife and family and vows never to drink again.

The hard work of a sober man is rewarded.

The family grows happy and prosperous in the shining light of father's reform.

German brewers circulated these colored advertisements extolling the virtues of lager beer to young children as well as adults. Courtesy: Dossin Great Lakes Museum.

COMPLIMENTS OF

GEORGE H. GIES,

16 Monroe Avenue,

DETROIT MICH.

AGAINST PROHIBITION   NO. 4.

The youth from school and study free,
Enjoys his Lager temperately

COMPLIMENTS OF

GEORGE H. GIES,

16 Monroe Avenue,

DETROIT MICH.

AGAINST PROHIBITION   NO. 5.

Refreshing Beer gives strength and health,
And smooths the rugged road to wealth.

Detroiters celebrated the end of World War I. Courtesy: Archives of Labor and Urban Affairs, Wayne State University

The capture and arrest of the Billingsley gang in September 1918 broke up the major whiskey smuggling ring that operated between Ohio and Michigan. Five carloads of whiskey were seized. Courtesy: Michigan State Archives.

Billy and "Ma" Sunday surrounded by ushers at a Detroit Prohibition Rally in the autumn of 1916. Thousands turned out for his evangelistic tirades against liquor. Courtesy: Burton Historical Collection.

The Reverend Billy Sunday, the charismatic temperance leader, is shown in one of his characteristic poses. Courtesy: *Detroit News.*

PROHIBITION IS A FARCE!
PROHIBITION IS HYPOCRISY!
PROHIBITION IS DEATH DEALING!
PROHIBITION IS CONFISCATION!
PROHIBITION IS AN EVIL---NOT A CURE!

COLORADO HAS PROVED IT SO.

Men are dying in Colorado because they drink "Boot-Leg" Whiskey.

The temperate man of yester-year is the man who is now dying in Colorado because he drinks vile "Boot-Leg" intoxicants.

THIS IS THE TYPE OF PROHIBITION THAT FANATICS WOULD FOIST ON MICHIGAN.

HOME RULE—THE CITY, VILLAGE and TOWN UNIT OF OPTION WOULD ALLOW EVERY COMMUNITY TO LICENSE AND REGULATE.

HOME RULE WOULD KEEP OUT DEATH DEALING "BOOTLEGGERS."

HOME RULE WOULD PREVENT CONFISCATION AND GRANT REGULATION.

THIS IS WHAT "COMMON CARRIERS" AND "AUTO BOOTLEGGERS" HAVE DONE TO COLORADO.

LET COLORADO'S PLIGHT BE A LESSON TO YOU.

VOTE TO KEEP THEM OUT OF MICHIGAN, ON

You will be handed two separate ballots. Vote them both like this:

| STATE PROHIBITION Amendment to ARTICLE XVI—Section 11 Vote "NO" | Yes | |
| | NO | X |

| HOME-RULE Amendment to ARTICLE VIII—Section 30 Vote "YES" | Yes | X |
| | No | |

This advertisement opposing the Michigan Prohibition Amendment appeared in the *Detroit Saturday Night* a few days before the fall elections, November 4, 1916.

Even before the Eighteenth Amendment took effect, opponents of Prohibition started a campaign for its repeal. Courtesy: Dossin Great Lakes Museum.

"The whole theory of prohibition is wrong. Live and let live. Be men and let us govern ourselves. We have but one hope and one dream — Freedom." *Clarence Darrow.*

THE "DRAGS"

"Prohibition would destroy approximately $300,000,000 Internal Revenue while the evils of intemperance would continue to exist." *Oscar W. Underwood*

This advertisement appeared in Detroit newspapers during the Prohibition campaign. Courtesy: Burton Historical Collections.

Putting the mortgage on the cradle.

Thirty-Six States Can Stop This By Constitutional Amendment

The saloon and the bartender were often the targets of Prohibitionists. This cartoon was one of a series published during the campaign for the Eighteenth Amendment. Courtesy: Library of Congress.

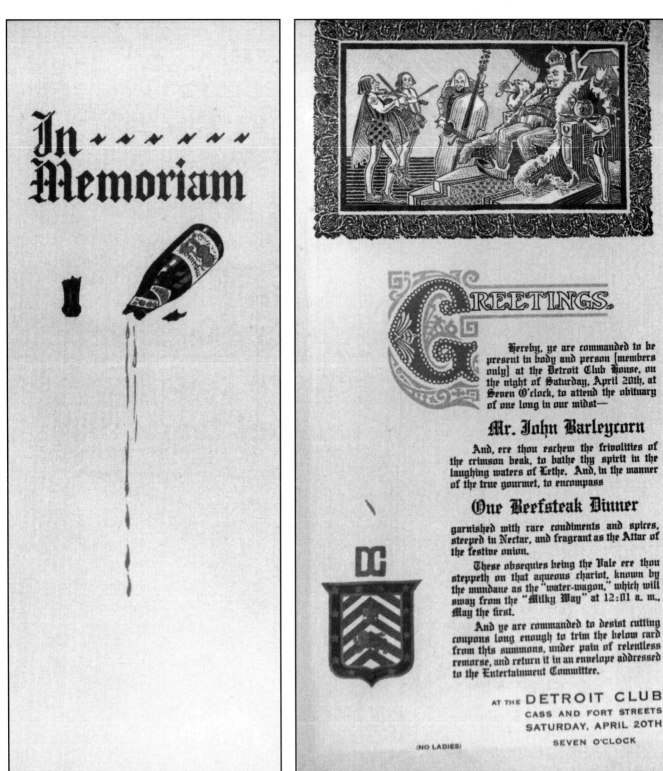

In Memoriam

GREETINGS.

Hereby, ye are commanded to be present in body and person [members only] at the Detroit Club House, on the night of Saturday, April 20th, at Seven O'clock, to attend the obituary of one long in our midst—

Mr. John Barleycorn

And, ere thou eschew the frivolities of the crimson beak, to bathe thy spirit in the laughing waters of Lethe. And, in the manner of the true gourmet, to encompass

One Beefsteak Dinner

garnished with rare condiments and spices, steeped in Nectar, and fragrant as the Attar of the festive onion.

These obsequies being the Vale ere thou steppeth on that aqueous chariot, known by the mundane as the "water-wagon," which will away from the "Milky Way" at 12:01 a. m., May the first.

And ye are commanded to desist cutting coupons long enough to trim the below card from this summons, under pain of relentless remorse, and return it in an envelope addressed to the Entertainment Committee.

AT THE DETROIT CLUB
CASS AND FORT STREETS
SATURDAY, APRIL 20TH
SEVEN O'CLOCK

(NO LADIES)

The Detroit Club hosted a special dinner to mark the fall of John Barleycorn on April 20, 1917. The club secretary also notified all members to remove liquor from their lockers immediately. Courtesy: Florence Livingstone Odell Ledyard.

The Music ～～～

Rendering (take it either way) all the classics, excepting:

L'Amour de Tres Rois (not a cigar)

Swan Song—*Pagliacci*

Hair-clipping Aria—*Samson et Delilah*

"Mimi" blowing out the candle—*La Boheme*

Balcony Scene (without the balcony)
—*Romeo and Juliet*

Bacchanal: "The Paper Drinking Cup"
(new version of the "Old Oaken
Bucket.")

Concluding with the popular dithyramb
"We Won't Go Home 'til Morning."

The Movie ～～～

The Power of the Petticoat
and
Sensored Features
By arrangement with Oliver Tabasco

A galaxy of Dazzling Dames, Vamping
Vamps and Silent Sirens

Theda—the Peerless One

Clara—the Incomparable

Daring Doug

Francis X—he of the lithe limbs

A pot-pourri of slap-sticks,
heroics, thrills.

Living Pictures ～～～

Peadish
and
Stanbody

In "The World's Greatest Physics"

posing as Gentlemen

(and a great many other things—

or what will you have)

Astounding   Amazing

Alluring

and everything like that.

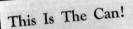

After Prohibition was passed in Michigan, the Stroh Brewery converted its plants to produce ice cream, ginger ale, near beer, and a Pure Hopped Malt Syrup. Courtesy: Stroh Archives.

THE EIGHTEENTH AMENDMENT

CANADA...THE BOOTLEGGERS' PARADISE
DETROIT...THEIR KLONDIKE

THE PASSAGE OF THE Eighteenth Amendment to the United States Constitution prohibiting the manufacture, sale, and consumption of alcoholic beverages passed on the national level just as easily as did a similar amendment in the state of Michigan. On June 11, 1917, the United States Senate adopted the amendment by an overwhelming majority after only thirteen hours of debate. The House of Representatives gave its approval on December 18, 1917, by a vote of 282 to 138. By January 1919 the necessary three-fourths of the states had ratified it. The Michigan state legislature had voted its approval on January 3, 1919, making it the sixteenth state to endorse the measure. However, it was not counted among the needed thirty-six states because of an error in the resolution adopting the amendment.[1]

The next action of Congress was the passage of the Volstead Act which provided for the enforcement of the Eighteenth Amendment. It defined "intoxicating liquors" as any liquor containing more than 0.5 percent alcohol, it permitted the manufacture of non-intoxicating cider and fruit juices for home use, and it allowed the sale of alcoholic beverages for medicinal, sacramental, and industrial purposes. The act allowed individuals to consume at home any liquor obtained legally before the passage of the amendment, and it provided penalties for the violation of the act. Although there was opposition to the provisions of the Volstead Act and scattered protest meetings and rallies were held, organized opposition was weak. Even Woodrow Wilson's veto was easily overridden.

In retrospect, the easy adoption of the Prohibition Amendment should come as no surprise. The "drys," as proponents of Prohibition were popularly called, were well financed and organized. With the support of distinguished community and business leaders, influential members of the clergy, and charismatic speakers like Billy Sunday, they campaigned on the "high moral road." The "wets," on the other hand, were poorly organized, and the reputation of recognized opponents of Prohibition—the saloon keepers, brewers, and distillers who were viewed as corruptors of state and local government —had been widely discredited. Even the opposition to the Volstead Act by the American Federation of Labor, which demanded that beer be exempt from Prohibition, received little support.

The entrance of the United States into the war with Germany added an important factor in winning support for Prohibition. During the war years, the federal government had greatly expanded its power over the daily lives of American citizens. Rationing was widely accepted as a necessary ingredient of the American war effort. The exclusive use of grain for foodstuffs for Allied soldiers rather than for alcoholic beverages also won public support. The anti–German sentiment in the United States resulted in open hostility toward brewers and distillers, many of whom were of German origin.[2]

The public response to the passage of the Eighteenth Amendment was predictable. It was heralded by drys as the beginning of a new era in American life. With rhetoric similar to that heard in Michigan three years earlier after passage of the state's Prohibition Amendment, supporters proclaimed that the winners were the American families, churches, schools, workers, and the American political system. The losers were criminals and drunks, saloon keepers, brewers and distillers, and corrupt politicians controlled by the liquor lobby. In reaction to the passage of the Eighteenth Amendment, the charismatic Billy Sunday characterized the euphoric spirit of the Prohibition leaders in his statement, "Good Bye John. You were God's worst enemy. You were hell's best friend. I hate you with a perfect hatred. I love to hate you. The reign of tears is over, the slums will soon be a memory; we will turn our prisons into factories and our jails into storehouses and corncribs. Men will walk upright now, women will smile, and children will laugh. Hell will be forever for rent."[3]

The new era began the morning of January 16, 1920. But, as Federick Lewis Allen, chronicler of the 1920s, observed, "Only gradually did the dry leaders, or Congress, or the public at large begin to perceive that the problem with which they had so light headedly grappled was a problem of gigantic proportions." [4]

The basic problem, it turned out, was the difficulty of shutting off the supply of liquor on the North American continent. It was recognized by some, based upon the experience of Michigan and other states that had earlier adopted dry laws, that a certain amount of beer, wine, and whiskey would be produced illegally in commercial breweries and distilleries and at home in stills. The smuggling of contraband liquor from European and Caribbean countries might also pose a minor problem but one that could be easily controlled. The Dominion of Canada, however, was the key to the enforcement of Prohibition in the United States. There was every indication that Canada, the scene of a strong Prohibition movement, would adopt controls over the use of liquor similar to those passed in the United States. After all, Canada had passed a Wartime Resource Act prohibiting the manufacture, sale, or consumption of alcoholic beverages, and the Prohibition movement in most of Canada had paralleled that in the United States. [5]

The clue to Canada's policies on Prohibition came in 1920 when the Wartime Prohibition Acts expired on January 1, 1920. The Parliament in Ottawa passed legislation authorizing each province to decide if Prohibition would continue. Ontario, along with other Canadian provinces, passed legislation continuing the policy of prohibiting the sale of liquor except for medicinal purposes. Quebec was the exception. It voted "wet," authorizing the sale and consumption of wine, beer, and hard liquor within the province.

The control of the manufacture, importation, and exportation of alcoholic beverages rested with the federal government in Ottawa. Without hesitation, it approved liquor production in all of the provinces, regardless of whether the provinces prohibited the sale of liquor, and the federal government immediately began to issue licenses to distilleries and breweries. In Ontario alone in 1920, twenty-nine breweries and sixteen distilleries were given approval to manufacture liquor. Several of the largest were located in southwestern Ontario near the Detroit River and the Michigan–Ontario waterway.

In the province of Ontario, which bordered on New York, Pennsylvania, Ohio, Michigan, and Minnesota, citizens were unable to purchase liquor from retail outlets, but they could legally order wine, beer, and whiskey from the province of Quebec and have it delivered to their homes for private consumption. There were no limits on the amount that could be ordered as long as it met these provisions.

There were other curious provisions of Canadian law. Windsor citizens, for example, could not purchase Hiram Walker liquor from the distillery in nearby Walkerville or in any Ontario outlet, but they could order Hiram Walker liquor that had been transported to Quebec and have it reshipped to Windsor.

Ontario court and police records attest to the abuses of the Canadian liquor policy and the manner in which it encouraged smuggling. During the first seven months of 1920, nine hundred thousand cases of liquor were shipped to Windsor and the surrounding cities of Sandwich, LaSalle, Riverside, and Ford for "personal use." One Windsor widow was called before a magistrate in July 1920 to explain her purchase of forty cases and nine barrels of Canadian whiskey over a six–month period. She explained that she developed a taste for the whiskey during the recent war when she became overwrought about the plight of Canadian soldiers. When the magistrate calculated her daily consumption of liquor at five quarts, he ordered her cache confiscated by authorities. Other Ontario residents, often joined by friends from Michigan, traveled to Quebec cities by automobile and truck and returned with cases of liquor for home use and resale.[6]

Another major loophole in Canadian liquor laws and regulations involved the export of liquor from distilleries and breweries in Ontario to foreign countries that did not have Prohibition. Under the provisions of this regulation, huge ship-

ments of liquor were scheduled for departure from Windsor daily for Barbados, Cuba, Mexico, and other foreign countries. Although the Canadian government levied a nine–dollar tax on each quart manufactured, to be refunded if proper documents were later presented proving delivery, this did not deter smuggling. The tax was merely added on to the price of the liquor.[7]

There were sources of liquor other than Canada. The two French islands in the mouth of the St. Lawrence River—Saint Pierre and Miquelon—became major outlets for contraband liquor, especially for Boston, New York, and other East Coast cities. Cuba, Barbados, and other Caribbean Islands also supplied liquor for smuggling. Mexico, with a long and isolated border, provided another base for bringing in contraband liquor. Ironically, much of the liquor from Mexico was manufactured in Canada, transported by ship and rail through the United States to Mexican outlets, and then smuggled into Texas, New Mexico, Arizona, and California.[8]

On the East Coast, the major method of smuggling involved ocean–going vessels which anchored offshore in international waters near Boston, New York, Miami, and other major coastal cities. Smaller boats came out from the mainland, purchased supplies of liquor, and ran the gauntlet of the U.S. Coast Guard to get their cargo into port. Hundreds of vessels were seized by authorities and their cargoes destroyed, but large numbers succeeded and supplied the demands of East Coast speakeasies and blind pigs.

In the early years of Prohibition the national media centered most of its attention on the smuggling operation off the East Coast, especially the role of Coast Guard vessels in capturing rumrunners. But they soon recognized that the main avenue was the smuggling of Canadian whiskey across the several thousand mile boundary between Canada and the United States stretching from Maine to Washington. Within that area the waterway separating Michigan and Ontario was the focal point for large–scale smuggling. An estimated 75 percent of liquor smuggled into the United States during Prohibition arrived along this route, especially through the thirty–mile stretch from Lake Erie to the St. Clair River, north of Lake St. Clair. The popular phrase, "The Windsor–Detroit Funnel" accurately described the main crossing point of smugglers.[9]

The Detroit River, running due north and then east for a total of twenty–eight miles from Lake Erie to Lake St. Clair, was a smuggler's paradise. The river was narrow, often less than a mile across, and could easily be crossed in a powerboat in less than five minutes. Numerous islands dotted the river providing hiding places for smugglers. Especially popular were Bois Blanc, Grosse Ile, Fighting Island, Belle

Isle, and Peche Island. All had excellent small harbors and inlets where smugglers could hide from the Coast Guard and police patrols. Roy A. Haynes, the national Prohibition director for the United States, accurately described this waterway in 1923 when he observed: "The Lord probably could have built a river better suited for rum–smuggling, but the Lord probably never did."[10]

The Canadian shoreline from Amherstburg to Tecumseh, east of Windsor, was ideally suited for smuggling. Several export docks where distillers and brewers were authorized to store thousands of cases of whiskey for reshipment were situated along this stretch of the river. Numerous rivers and creeks with boat slips and marinas flowed into the Detroit River, and the miles of tall marsh grass gave additional cover from detection by authorities. On the Canadian shoreline it was aptly observed, "there are several of the most prosperous of all the numerous border 'filling–stations' for American Bootleggers."[11]

Conditions on the United States side of the river also aided smugglers. Much of the shoreline between Toledo and Detroit was deserted or sparsely settled and had landing places for small boats with drafts too shallow for the large Coast Guard vessels. A string of cities and towns along the river also had excellent harbor facilities—Gibraltar, Trenton, Riverview, Wyandotte, Ecorse, and River Rouge. These communities not only had marinas, fishing docks, canals, and boat slips, but hundreds of shoreline residents had private boat houses and docks. Many of these facilities were connected by underground tunnels to residences located several hundred feet inland. Although these intricate underground passages had not been built initially for smuggling, enterprising home owners soon recognized the unusual opportunities they offered to quickly unload and conceal contraband liquor.

The waterway separating the cities of Windsor and Detroit was ideal for rumrunning. The river was narrow and both sides had ample dock facilities with a large number of boat slips or canals. Belle Isle, a city recreational park, located only a few hundred yards from Windsor, could be easily reached by rowboats and power vessels. Law enforcement officials stationed in downtown office buildings could easily observe rumrunners racing across the river, but, by the time police patrols arrived at the landing sites, the liquor had been unloaded and carried away to warehouses and other hiding places. The opening of the Ambassador Bridge between Detroit and Windsor in November 1929 and the Detroit–Windsor Tunnel a year later provided even more opportunities for smuggling.

Lake St. Clair, which stretched thirty miles from the Detroit River to the St. Clair River, also provided a haven for smug-

glers. Its sheer size gave rumrunners unusual opportunities to evade the police and Prohibition officials. Its numerous islands and miles of deserted shoreline ideally concealed boats laden with contraband. The lake was also popular among thousands of fishermen and pleasure boaters which made the detection of smugglers extremely difficult. It was virtually impossible to stop and search every boat. Furthermore, hundreds of boathouses, marinas, canals, and docking facilities along the United States' side of the lake also facilitated the smuggling operation.

The narrow St. Clair River, running about thirty–five miles to Port Huron, was also a paradise for smugglers. Like the Detroit River, its narrow span and miles of deserted, sparsely settled shoreline enabled power boats to cross within a few minutes and drop off contraband liquor at marinas, boathouses, and docks located the length of the river. From facilities in Algonac, Marine City, St. Clair, Marysville, and Port Huron, automobiles and trucks transported the liquor to other cities in Michigan and the Midwest.

The final links in the smuggler's chain along the Michigan–Ontario waterway were Lake Huron and the St. Mary's River. Although the amount smuggled on these waterways did not compare to the Detroit River–Lake St. Clair segment, it was nonetheless significant and met the demands of thousands of residents of northern Michigan and Illinois.

Within hours after the Volstead Act went into effect on January 17, 1920, the smuggling of liquor into the United States began, first on a small scale. Some Canadian citizens already had been making plans for rumrunning well in advance. By June 1, 1920, Canadian Customs officials, for example, had noticed the sharp increase in the application for motor boat licenses among Windsor and other Ontario residents.[12] Also, large orders for liquor had been received at Windsor area export docks for shipment to numerous foreign ports. Without question Detroit area residents, who had been deeply involved a few months earlier in smuggling liquor from Ohio, were also primed for new opportunities—this time across the narrow waterway separating Michigan and Ontario. The roster of new rumrunners included many of the fishing enthusiasts and pleasure boaters who not only had vessels but who were intimately familiar with the waterway.

Rumrunning in the early months of Prohibition was often a family affair. In jalopies and small boats fathers, sons, cousins, and other relatives crossed the ice and water, purchased from fifteen to twenty cases of Canadian whiskey, and returned to their communities in the metropolitan area. At first, to avoid detection, the rumrunning expeditions took place at

night. Later, when powerboats were used, rumrunners rushed across at all hours of the day.

Windsor residents also capitalized upon the huge profits in rumrunning. In 1920 alone, 900,000 cases of whiskey were shipped into the Windsor area from Quebec, most of which were destined for the Detroit market. An estimated 25 percent of Windsor's residents were involved in smuggling in 1920. Court records support this estimate. Between January and July of 1920, Windsor courts collected $250,000 in fines from boaters caught smuggling. Nevertheless, despite the efforts of Ontario enforcement officials, the annual sales in 1920 totaled nearly $219 million from Canadian whiskey and an additional $30 million from the sale of wine. As Marty Gervais, the historian of Windsor Prohibition, has pointed out, many Windsorites became millionaires during the 1920s and many of the community's palatial mansions were built with profits from rumrunning.[13]

The techniques of smuggling liquor into Michigan changed as the years passed in the 1920s. Smugglers introduced high speed and larger boats which could easily outrun the police boats. By 1923, when organized criminal gangs entered the smuggling operation, they used more sophisticated techniques. Rumrunners developed various devices such as flashing colored lights, flares, clothes hung on lines, telephones, and radios to signal gang members on the opposite side of the river that the coast was clear. They also used signals, especially on Lake St. Clair, to warn rumrunners to change their routes if police patrols were near the designated landing place.[14]

Criminal gangs also developed methods to speed up the delivery of contraband liquor and to avoid jeopardy of the organized effort. The system worked like clockwork. One group arranged the purchase of liquor at the export docks along the river; another crew transported the liquor across to a designated location; a third team quickly picked up the cases of whiskey and transported them to warehouses; and later another arranged the shipments to speakeasies in Detroit, Chicago, and other midwestern cities. Armed guards accompanied the caravans that sped to Chicago and other midwestern cities.[15]

Organized gangs with strong financial backing bribed federal, state, and local police officials. On some days, at designated times, police patrols had to be cancelled because all officers called in sick. Some police officers were engaged in rumrunning activities privately or were on the payrolls of organized gangs. Hundreds of police and public officials were indicted and convicted for their roles in smuggling. Even honest enforcement agents paid a penalty for their actions. Their dishonest colleagues ostracized and threatened them, often forcing them to request reassignment or early retirement.[16]

The methods used by rumrunners to transport contraband liquor into Michigan depended upon several factors. In the early days of Prohibition, when the federal and local enforcement agencies were hopelessly inadequate, rumrunners used all sections of the waterway at all times of the day and night. After 1923, when the federal agencies stepped up their surveillance and as Michigan and Detroit police added more patrol boats and officers, smugglers became more careful and selective in planning illicit crossings.

The weather and condition of the waterway also had to be considered carefully. During winter months, when Lake St. Clair and sections of the Detroit and St. Clair rivers were covered with ice, jalopies and trucks with doors removed for safety reasons crossed the frozen span to transport liquor. Sometimes single vehicles crossed the ice, but more often they crossed in convoys for protection against hijackers and accidents. Automobiles often dragged sleds filled with cases of liquor across the ice, thereby spreading the weight over a larger section of the ice. In February 1930, during one of the coldest periods of the century, the *Detroit News* reported a convoy of seventy–five automobiles leaving the export docks in

Amherstburg, Ontario, heading for Michigan via Bois Blanc and Grosse Ile.[17]

Lake St. Clair was also a popular winter crossing point, especially because of its size and the safer condition of the ice. Ice boats often replaced the jalopies which, despite their more limited cargo capacity, could easily outrun police vehicles. They were able to cross in about ten to fifteen minutes. Small–time entrepreneurs skated across the ice dragging sleds laden with several cases of whiskey. As laborious as this method of smuggling was, it nonetheless yielded enough profit to make it worthwhile. A *New York Times* reporter described the scene in the winter of 1925: "On Lake St. Clair a new and strange phenomenon that rushes on the wings of a nor'easter through the friendly darkness, bringing contraband liquor from the Canadian shore."[18] During spring, summer, and fall, when ice left the waterway, boats transported the liquor. They ranged from small rowboats to large power–driven vessels capable of running circles around police boats. Tens of thousands of licensed boats were in operation when Prohibition began in 1920—mostly pleasure and fishing boats. The number quickly increased as smuggling became more profitable.

The fact that the Coast Guard and police captured and confiscated thousands of vessels did not stop or even deter smuggling. Replacements could easily be found. Long before Prohibition Detroit had become one of the country's leading manufacturers of marine engines and power boats and could easily meet the demand of smugglers. Furthermore, thousands of the confiscated rumrunner boats were sold at auction and within days repurchased by rumrunners. In 1920 Detroit Police seized the *Tennessee II*, one of the fastest vessels on the lakes, in the process of unloading contraband liquor. They soon recommissioned it as a police vessel and used it in the campaign against smugglers.[19]

Smugglers also developed underwater crossings. They dragged huge sleds, filled with cases of liquor, across the river bottom with the aid of steel cables and pulleys. Similar mechanisms were used to haul underwater torpedo–like tubes and comparable containers filled with forty gallons of whiskey. Detroit Police patrols discovered such a device, operating between Peche Island and Alter Road in Detroit, in 1931.[20] Mud Island, located off Ecorse, was the site of a similar ploy. From a partially submerged houseboat underwater cables pulled containers of whiskey to a boathouse in Ecorse.[21] The *New York Times* reported in May 1920 that smugglers were using an electrically controlled torpedo with capacities of fifty gallons of whiskey to cross the Detroit River, landing at a site east of Woodward Avenue. According to news reports, it took five minutes to cross the river.[22] Another group of enterprising smugglers had laid a pipe under the Detroit River connecting a Windsor distillery outlet and a Detroit bottling plant. According to the news account, the illegal device was discovered and dismantled when a mechanic, who had been called in to repair the pump, notified authorities.[23]

Smugglers began to utilize airplanes after the "Prohibition Navy" became more effective later in the 1920s, in spite of drawbacks such as the small cargo space, the limited number of air fields, and the necessity of flying during daylight hours. Nevertheless, when the Prohibition Navy curtailed river smuggling, rumrunning by air increased sharply. In 1930 two smuggling syndicates operated thirty planes transporting an estimated $100,000 worth of liquor a month. Pilots from nearby Selfridge Air Field, when not on duty, earned extra money transporting contraband liquor.[24]

Railroads were also used extensively to transport liquor into Michigan from Ontario. Thousands of railroad cars crossed the Detroit and St. Clair rivers daily, via the two tunnels and on the railroad ferries that regularly plied the rivers. They carried liquor hidden under cargoes of grain, wood, Christmas trees, or other bulk freight and undetected by the short–staffed customs patrols. In other instances, grain or other legitimate cargoes had been removed from freight cars and replaced by thousands of cases of liquor. Bogus seals were substituted, allowing the cars to pass undetected to Detroit, Chicago, and other cities.[25]

Accurate records do not exist on how much contraband liquor came into Michigan illegally via railroad but, from all indications, it was very substantial. According to the *Detroit News*, at least one half of the liquor smuggled into the states arrived by rail from Canada. The *New York Times* substantiated these figures. It reported that in 1923 the rail freight cars delivered an estimated eight hundred cases of Canadian beer into Detroit daily. Several years later the *Times* reported that huge quantities of hard liquor and beer arrived in Detroit by railroad. Between April 1, 1927, and March 31, 1928, the figures tally more than 3.3 million gallons of liquor valued at $20 million being shipped by rail into the Detroit area.[26]

The automotive and passenger ferries that operated at numerous points in the Michigan–Ontario waterway provided other opportunities for smugglers. Using techniques mastered earlier during Michigan's Prohibition in 1917 and 1918, smugglers rebuilt automobiles and trucks to provide hiding places for liquor, installing new fuel tanks with compartments for liquor and fuel and adding false roofs and hidden compartments under seats to hide contraband liquor. On occasion, hearses were even used to smuggle liquor in caskets along with, or in place of, the deceased.[27]

Animal owners used their pets as ploys. Customs officials in Detroit finally discovered such a ruse after noticing one passenger bringing his dog across on the ferry each week. A careful search of the dog's cage revealed a dozen quarts of high quality Canadian whiskey hidden in a false compartment at the bottom of the cage.[28]

Individual passengers on ferries also smuggled liquor into Michigan, although not on the extensive scale that boats, planes, and railroad cars did. A *New York Times* writer, covering the Windsor–Detroit rumrunning scene, reported that Detroit employed stenographers and secretaries who commuted daily from Windsor, often carrying liquor in lunch boxes or strapped to their persons. They were "aided and abetted by their Canadian fathers and brothers" and overlooked by customs agents who "do not molest the flappers or working girls earning a living."[29] Ferry passengers also donned rubber chest protectors similar to those worn by baseball catchers and umpires, hot water bottles, and overcoats with a series of pockets sewn on the inside lining, each large enough to hold a bottle of whiskey. Smugglers also employed some bizarre devices. For instance, in the summer of 1920 Customs inspectors noticed an increase in the number of egg baskets ferry passengers carried into the United States. This ploy was soon exposed when one passenger accidentally dropped his basket of eggs while departing the ferry. It was not the odor of rotten eggs that alert-

ed the customs officer, but rather the scent of high–grade scotch whiskey. The egg shells had been carefully emptied, filled with liquor, and resealed.[30]

In 1929 and 1930 new avenues for rumrunning appeared with the opening of the Ambassador Bridge and the Detroit–Windsor Tunnel, respectively. Automobile and truck traffic increased sharply as a result of this more convenient means of crossing the Detroit River. Despite customs inspections, hundreds of thousands of cases of wine, beer, and whiskey found their way into Detroit and other midwestern cities via the new bridge and tunnel.

By 1930, despite increased staff and facilities, the media and concerned public officials raised the questions: Why couldn't smuggling be curtailed and the Volstead Act strictly enforced, especially after a decade of experience? Why was it so easy to get hard liquor, beer, and wine in local speakeasies and blind pigs and have unlimited supplies of booze delivered to your home? In retrospect, the reasons are obvious. Not only was the Michigan–Ontario waterway long and difficult to patrol, but the large number of smugglers had developed extremely sophisticated and effective methods of smuggling. Furthermore, the astronomical profits from rumrunning and the relatively minor penalties for illegal liquor convictions did little to discourage smuggling. A *New York Times* reporter put the matter of smuggling along the Detroit River in clear perspective when he concluded, "The United States government would have to employ an inspector to every man and woman and child who crosses the ferry from Windsor to Detroit. It would have to line the shore for thirty miles with armed guards to hold up and search every craft that tries to land and then it would not begin to make serious inroads on the operation of the rumrunners." The astute reporter summed up the Prohibition scene on the Detroit River with the headline, "Canada is the Bootleggers' Paradise and Detroit their Klondike."[31]

WHITEFISH BAY

Sault St. Marie

ST. MARYS RIVER

St. Joseph I.

NORTH CHANNEL

Port Dolomite
Les Cheneaux Is.
Drummond I.
Cockburn I.
Mackinac I.

Bois Blanc I.

Mackinaw City

Cheboygan

Manitoulin Island

INTERNATIONAL BOUNDARY

LITTLE TRAVERSE BAY

Forty Mile Pt.

Rogers City

GEORGIAN BAY

Presque Isle
Stoneport

Rockport

Alpena

THUNDER BAY

Harrisville

LAKE HURON

Oscoda

East Tawas

Pte. aux Barques

Port Austin

Ontario

Port Albert

Harbor Beach

Goderich

Bay City

Port Sanilac

LAKE ONTARIO

Saginaw

Hamilton

Port Weller

NIAGARA RIVER

Lakeport

WELLAND CANAL

Port Huron

Sarnia

Port Dovero

Port Colborne

St. Clair

Buffalo

Michigan

Marine City

Algonac

ST. CLAIR RIVER

Port Stanley

Port Burwell

Dunkirk

Mt Clemens

DETROIT RIVER

LAKE ST. CLAIR

Rondeau Hbr.

Detroit

Windsor

ROUGE R.

Kingsville

LAKE ERIE

Erie

INTERNATIONAL BOUNDARY

Conneaut

Monroe

Ashtabula

Fairport

Mentor Harbor

Toledo

Port Clinton

Sandusky

Cleveland

Huron

Vermilion

Lorain

Rocky River

Ohio

The hundreds of miles of waterway between Ontario and New York, Ohio, and Michigan offered limitless opportunities for smugglers. Millions of gallons of Canadian beer, wine, and whiskey were smuggled from Ontario into the United States. The Detroit River–Lake St. Clair route was used most heavily by rumrunners. Courtesy: U.S. Army Corps of Engineers.

Despite attempts of Ontario temperance leaders to stop its circulation, this postcard was widely distributed in Ontario and Michigan. Courtesy: *Windsor Star.*

Windsor and Detroit were less than a mile apart on many sections of the Detroit River. The skyline of Detroit is seen here from Ouelette Street in Windsor. Courtesy: Burton Historical Collection.

Numerous rivers, streams, and creeks flowed into the Detroit River providing excellent cover for rumrunners. Courtesy: C. H. Gervais.

Whiskey shipments were piled on the ice on the Canadian side of the river awaiting the arrival of rumrunners. Courtesy: C. H. Gervais.

Rumrunner loaded at Windsor Export Dock and ready to leave for Detroit, September 8, 1928. Courtesy: *Detroit News.*

The Ontario Export Docks at Amherstburg shipped out millions of cases of Canadian whiskey and beer during the 1920s. The name of this rumrunner has been covered with a tarp to avoid detection, June 27, 1929. Courtesy: *Detroit News.*

Rumrunner leaving export dock at Amherstburg, June 22, 1929. Courtesy: *Detroit News.*

This rumrunner, out of Sandusky, Ohio, was rebuilt to facilitate the loading and unloading of contraband liquor. The *Neptune* was captured by the U.S. Coast Guard in June 1929. Courtesy: The Press Collection, Cleveland State University.

A lookout on a Canadian dock uses binoculars to get the signal from American side. A rumrunner is loaded and ready to cross the Detroit River. Courtesy: *Detroit News, Windsor Star.*

A *Detroit News* photographer hidden in a coal elevator at the foot of Riopelle Street captured the scene of the unloading of a rumrunner (out of sight) near downtown Detroit. A smuggler's scout car in foreground is on the lookout for police. It took only five minutes to unload and leave the site, April 1929. Courtesy: *Detroit News.*

Three hundred cases of liquor were salvaged by rumrunners from a boat stuck on a sand bar, October 2, 1925. Courtesy: *Windsor Star*.

Smugglers often used women and children as decoys. These rumrunners are seen arriving in Ecorse with loads of Canadian liquor. Courtesy: Dossin Great Lakes Museum.

Jalopies were used to pick up contraband Canadian liquor from vessels in Lake St. Clair. Courtesy: Dossin Great Lakes Museum.

Rumrunners proudly display cargo of smuggled Canadian whiskey. Courtesy: C. H. Gervais.

This aerial view of the Detroit River between Amherstburg, Ontario, and Grosse Ile shows the route of rumrunners during winter. Courtesy: *Detroit News.*

Old jalopies (dubbed the Whiskey Six) were used to carry liquor across the ice during harsh winters. The doors were often removed to aid drivers if they had to jump out quickly. Courtesy: *Windsor Star.*

A caravan of jalopies reach Grosse Ile from Amherstburg, February 15, 1930. Courtesy: *Detroit News.*

This beer–laden smuggler's truck was too heavy for the ice on Lake St. Clair in the winter of 1933. Several Grosse Pointe residents walked or skated out to witness the accident. Courtesy: *Detroit News.*

Lake St. Clair was especially popular for smuggling during cold winters when thick ice covered the lakes and rivers. Trucks with special tracks were ideal for hauling sleds piled with sacks of whiskey across the lake. Courtesy: Dossin Great Lakes Museum.

The completion of the Ambassador Bridge between Detroit and Windsor in November 1929 offered further opportunities for smuggling Canadian liquor into the U.S. The cables were raised on August 8, 1928. Courtesy: Burton Historical Collection.

Several automobile ferries that operated between Windsor and Detroit and other border cities carried tens of thousands of vehicles daily. Autos and trucks were often rebuilt to hide liquor. Courtesy: Dossin Great Lakes Museum.

The Detroit–Windsor Tunnel opened in 1930. Thousands of automobiles and trucks, many with hidden cargoes of liquor, crossed daily. Courtesy: Dossin Great Lakes Museum.

Smugglers had to be on the look-out for hijackers as well as the police. A hijacked rumrunner's auto was abandoned on Belle Isle. Courtesy: Dossin Great Lakes Museum.

The new bridge connecting Detroit and Belle Isle opened in 1923 and was used extensively by rum-runners who picked up liquor smuggled on to the island. Foggy nights were ideal for smuggling. Courtesy: Dossin Great Lakes Museum.

Trucks like these were used to transport smuggled Canadian whiskey from Detroit to Chicago and other cities in the Midwest. Courtesy: The Press Collection, Cleveland State University.

A truck is loading beer from a commercial still in Detroit, May 26, 1929. Courtesy: *Detroit News*.

Despite limited cargo space and the lack of safe airfields, airplanes were used extensively by smugglers. By 1930, when the U.S. Coast Guard and police patrols reduced river smuggling, planes were used to carry $100,000 worth of liquor each month. Ralph Capone, brother of the notorious Al, owned a fleet of twenty rumrunning airplanes. Courtesy: *Detroit News;* Dossin Great Lakes Museum.

U.S. Customs officials are seizing 720 quarts of liquor and wines from a funeral hearse, August 11, 1929. Courtesy: *Detroit News.*

A Detroit reporter demonstrates how liquor was sold on the streets of Detroit. Similar contraptions were used to smuggle liquor on ferries into Michigan. Courtesy: *Detroit News.*

"Nothing to declare" was the answer given to customs officials. Specially made coats with inside pockets, casts strapped around legs, and sometimes bottles and flasks of liquor in boots allowed women to smuggle several gallons of whiskey into Detroit on each trip. Courtesy: *Windsor Star.*

Brick door stops, each concealing a quart of whiskey, were discovered by accident by customs officials. Courtesy: Cleveland Public Library.

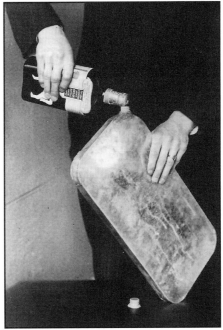

Watermelons, hot water bottles, and metal containers were often used to smuggle liquor. Courtesy: Cleveland Public Library; *Detroit News.*

Mrs. Nell Rhoades posed for a *Detroit Times* photographer in the 1930s showing how young women smuggled liquor on a Windsor–Detroit Ferry. Courtesy: Mrs. Nell Rhoades.

An ankle flask for the female tippler, 1922. Courtesy: Library of Congress.

Hundreds of thousands of cases of Canadian whiskey were smuggled via railroad freight cars. The Michigan Central Railroad Tunnel and railroad ferries transported hundreds of cars daily between Detroit and Windsor. Courtesy: Library of Congress.

A Canadian Pacific freight car is being loaded by smugglers for shipment to the U.S. Liquor was often hidden among grain and other produce. Official seals were broken and replaced by smugglers to avoid detection by customs officials. Courtesy: *Windsor Star.*

Liquor is being loaded on a speedboat from an export dock near Windsor. Courtesy: *Windsor Star.*

A federal agent inspects a freight car filled with contraband whiskey.
Courtesy: The Press Collection, Cleveland State University.

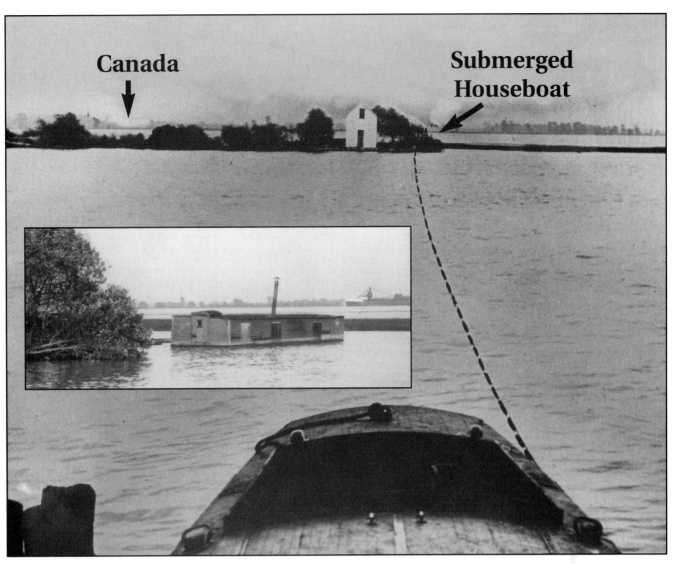

Canada

Submerged
Houseboat

Cables were used to transport cylinders of whiskey from a partially sunken houseboat off Mud Island in the Detroit River to a boat house in Ecorse. Courtesy: *Detroit News.*

U.S. Border Patrol inspectors discovered and confiscated this steel cable which ran from Peche Island, Ontario, to a cottage near the foot of Alter Road in Detroit. A motor–driven windlass dragged the huge metal cylinders, filled with thirty gallons of whiskey, across the river bottom. Courtesy: National Archives; *Detroit Free Press.*

3

DETROIT DURING PROHIBITION
THE MOTOR CITY REVOLUTION IN MANNERS, MORALS, AND MONEY

B Y THE MID 1920s, THE metropolitan Detroit area had become the focal point for the rumrunning business between Canada and the United States. The thirst of millions of midwesterners could be quenched by bootleggers operating across the narrow Detroit River and over the major highways leading out of Detroit. But by no means were Detroit residents deprived of beer, wine, and whiskey because of market demands from other areas in the Midwest. Hundreds of thousands of gallons of choice Canadian liquor remained in Detroit for restaurants, speakeasies, blind pigs, and delivery to homes, clubs, and excursion vessels. In addition, the local Detroit market was serviced by home and com-

mercial stills, distilleries, and breweries. Whereas the main industry of Detroit during the 1920s was the production of automobiles, the liquor industry—the smuggling and distribution of Canadian whiskey and manufacture of wine, beer, and hard liquor—ranked second. Tens of thousands of Detroit and Michigan residents owed their livelihoods to this illegal activity.

Detroit was neither alone nor unique in its blatant violation of the Volstead Act. Rumrunning was rampant along the 18,700–mile border surrounding the United States, and New York City and other East Coast cities were enmeshed in the smuggling and illegal consumption of liquor. However, Detroit stood out because of its location in the center of the main avenue of rumrunning from Canada, where an estimated 75 percent of illegal liquor entered the United States.[1]

The questions have often been asked: Why Detroit? Why Michigan? How could it happen in a state that overwhelmingly adopted statewide Prohibition in 1916 and gave strong support to the Eighteenth Amendment in 1918? What changes had taken place between 1916 and 1920 that led to such blatant violation of federal, state, and local laws? What was happening in Detroit and other Michigan cities during the twenties which might give answer to these perplexing questions?

THE ROARING TWENTIES

The 1920s, when the national experiment in Prohibition was in effect, witnessed profound changes in the way in which Americans lived, worked, and spent their leisure time. The disillusionment following the breakdown in peace negotiations at the end of World War I and the so–called "return to normalcy" which characterized the decade were factors in the pervasive violation of the provisions of the Volstead Act by so many Americans. Detroit area residents located along the border, the scene of the most intense and active smuggling in the country, were deeply influenced by these changes.[2]

The popular phrase "The Prosperous

Twenties" applied especially to the city of Detroit, located in the center of the largest smuggling operation in the United States. During this decade, the population of Detroit rose from 993,678 in 1920 to 1,568,662 in 1930, ranking it fourth in size in the nation both times. Most of the foreign–born immigrants came from Canada, Poland, England, Italy, and Scotland. The African–American population rose from 60,082 to 169,453. The migration from the rural south also increased significantly, although not in the volume of the later decades. The geographic size of the city of Detroit also expanded from 82.55 square miles in 1917 to 140 square miles in 1930, and the communities surrounding Detroit also witnessed similar growth.[3]

The sharp rise in population reflected the expanding economy of the Detroit area. Detroit, widely recognized for its role as the "Arsenal of Democracy" during World War I, produced airplanes, liberty engines, trucks, tanks, shells and other products needed by Allied forces. Following the war a period of adjustment and a depression lasted until 1923. Detroit soon reestablished itself as a world business center, dominated by the production of automobiles. By 1925 the automobile industry centered around General Motors, Ford, and Chrysler—all based in the Detroit area. The new Ford Rouge Plant and the replacement of the Model T with the Model A assured jobs for thousands of Ford workers, and the rising airplane industry also provided jobs for thousands of Detroit–area residents.

The skyline of Detroit changed significantly during the 1920s. Skyscrapers erected in the downtown area dwarfed the older office buildings, stores, and banks. The Buhl Building opened in 1925, followed by the Macabees Building and the Barlum Tower in 1927 and the Penobscot Building in 1928. The year 1929 saw the completion of the Guardian, David Stott, and *Detroit Times* buildings. The New Center area of Detroit expanded in 1928 with the addition of the Fisher Building, located across Grand Boulevard from the General Motors headquarters that was completed in 1922. Both buildings were designed by Albert Kahn.

New theaters and cultural centers also opened in the 1920s, including the Detroit Public Library, the Detroit Institute of Art, and the Henry Ford Museum & Greenfield Village in nearby Dearborn. The Masonic Auditorium and the Cass, State, United Artists, and Fisher Theaters opened in the mid–1920s, joined in 1928 by the Fox Theater with its capacity for five thousand patrons and its unparalleled decor. Hundreds of hotels and apartment houses were constructed during this decade, including the Book Cadillac Hotel in 1924. In this decade of "lush prosperity" Detroit ranked third after New York and Chicago in the construction of movie palaces, office buildings, and hotels.[4]

The atmosphere in the homes of Detroiters changed dramatically in August 1920 when WWJ became the first radio station in the United States to offer regularly scheduled programs. With the use of headsets and later radio loud-speakers, Detroiters tuned in on newscasts, concerts, and popular music. Special events, like the burial of the unknown soldier in Arlington National Cemetery, were heard over WWJ by citizens in their homes!

Sporting events, always popular among Detroiters, were especially so during Prohibition. The Detroit Tigers, with heroes like Ty Cobb and Harry Heilman, attracted thousands. Scores of new golf courses sprang up to meet the demands of this growing sport, and power boat racing, led by Gar Wood, who won the Harmsworth Racing Trophy in 1920 in *Miss America Two,* was popular in Detroit.[5]

Like New York, Boston, Chicago, and other sections of the country, fads and crazes found their way into the lives of Detroiters. Ouija and Mah Jongg, crossword puzzles, and auction bridge suddenly became especially popular in Detroit. Bathing beauty contests, featuring the one–piece form–fitting bathing suit, spread from Atlantic City in 1921 to Detroit and the Midwest. The one–step Charleston and Black Bottom were popular dances of the 1920s, and in April 1923, the Majestic Theater in Detroit held a marathon dance which lasted ninety–six and a half hours. The dance craze soon spread nationwide. This "flapper" age also witnessed the introduction of "talking pictures" in Detroit in 1926.[6]

A revolution in morals and manners, especially among the younger generation of Detroiters and counterparts throughout the United States, characterized this remarkable decade. Led largely by the sons and daughters of well–to–do Americans, the changes soon affected all citizens of all ages and of various economic backgrounds. Returning veterans from the war in Europe first questioned and challenged traditional values, followed by young American women, who had only just received suffrage and were anxious to alter their traditional family roles. With the introduction of new labor–saving appliances for the home, women increasingly had more time to devote to outside and community activities.

The attire of women also changed radically—shorter skirts revealed kneecaps, then short–sleeved dresses came into vogue, corsets were abandoned, and cosmetics, especially rouge and lipstick, became status symbols for the emancipated woman. Sigmund Freud's influence on many directly affected dating behavior between young men and women. Smoking cigarettes had long been accepted for men, but suddenly in the 1920s, women—even "nice" girls—openly and defiantly took up the habit. Even more drastic was the popular practice of drinking among well–to–do young women. They frequented speakeasies and blind pigs, often without chaperones or dates, and were accepted in taverns and old–time saloons, which earlier had not allowed women.[7]

Late afternoon cocktails became a tradition, as did serving drinks before dinner. At dances in hotel ballrooms, it was usually the custom to reserve a hotel room for drinking. As Frederick Lewis Allen, the historian of the 1920s, reported, "Drinking became the 'thing to do.'"[8] He also observed that although Prohibition had reduced drinking among workers and college students, the use of liquor by the prosperous and upper classes increased sharply and moreover established standards for acceptable behavior.[9]

In his masterful account of the Roaring Twenties, Allen in *Only Yesterday* described the new drinking habits of young men and women from a national point of view. His observation applied accurately to the situation in the Detroit area as well. From all indications, including newspaper accounts, police blotters, and court records, young Detroiters joined the older generation in violating the Volstead Act. They became steady customers of their favorite speakeasies and clubs, and they were not afraid of the publicity if arrested. In fact, frequenting a blind pig and being arrested was a status symbol to many.

THE SPEAKEASIES

"Joe sent me" was the popular phrase used during Prohibition to gain entrance into a speakeasy, blind pig, or joint. Every major city in Michigan and most small towns and rural communities had establishments in which trusted citizens could gain entrance and buy a shot of whiskey, a bottle of beer, or a glass of wine. Cocktails and mixed drinks were served in the more prestigious watering holes, especially in those that catered to women.

Detroit, the urban center of Michigan, had the largest number of speakeasies. In 1923 Detroit Police recorded about 3,000, but an additional 7,000 operated without the knowledge of the police. By 1925 the number had increased to 15,000, and by 1928, according to the *Detroit News*, the number ranged from 16,000 to 25,000 blind pigs.[10]

They were located in all sections of the metropolitan area, in downtown business districts, in wealthy residential communities, and in the low–income working–class sections of Detroit and surrounding cities. All types of buildings housed speakeasies. In fact, many restaurants and taverns that operated prior to Prohibition continued to serve liquor illegally to patrons until the repeal in 1933. Usually such establishments had separate facilities for trusted patrons, often on a second floor, in the basement, or a back room, monitored by a guard or bouncer. Hotels set aside special areas for their trusted drinking patrons, sometimes in rooms adjacent to dining facilities. For dances, balls, weddings, and other special events separate hotel suites were reserved for serving drinks. Business firms often served as "fronts" for speakeasies. In one downtown Detroit office the sign "Attorney–at–Law" had nothing to do with the legal profession. Rather than receiving legal services, the "clients" were served liquor. A downtown Turkish bath house, a tire store, and a grain and feed store competed with nearby barbershops, candy stores, meat markets, drug stores, and even a church basement for the sale of alcoholic refreshments.

Speakeasies prospered in residential sections of metropolitan Detroit and in surrounding suburbs. The Blossom Heath on Jefferson Avenue in St. Clair Shores and the Aniwa Club on Van Dyke, off East Jefferson, catered to the wealthy citizens of the Grosse Pointes. The Chesterfield Inn, Club Royale, Doc Brady's, Lefty Clark's, and D'Emilo's French Club also catered to the well–to–do. Downtown Detroit also had its favorites as well; Log

Cabin Inn on Woodward, Modena Inn on East Jefferson, Garage Inn on Grand River, the Manconi Cafe on Griswold, the Waiters and Waitresses Club on East Adams, and the Deutsches Haus on Mack Avenue were well known to a generation of Detroiters.[11] The Woodbridge Tavern, still a popular restaurant located just east of the Renaissance Center, served liquid refreshments to a large group of regular patrons during Prohibition.

Less pretentious but equally popular were the local speakeasies found in all sections of the area; in the basements of residences, in garages located in alleys, in the lofts of commercial buildings, and in the back rooms of ice cream parlors and party stores. Enterprising smugglers did not overlook rural areas. Several of the farmhouses located along Six, Seven, and Eight Mile Roads in Detroit were promptly converted into speakeasies catering to commuting motorists.[12]

The owners and operators of speakeasies varied according to the location and volume of business. Many were family affairs, catering to local clientele. Criminal gangs who were involved in the smuggling of liquor from Canada or who operated commercial stills in the Detroit area owned a significant number of these speakeasies and provided them with protection from local police and rival gangs. Independent operators of blind pigs needed connections with criminal gangs to assure prompt delivery of liquor. Local police were often on the payroll of speakeasies to assure protection from raids or violence from rival gangs.

The huge profits gained from operating a blind pig and the ease of securing a steady supply of liquor attracted many investors. Not only were the profits substantial, but the practice of diluting whiskey increased them even further. Even citizens with little money opened speakeasies. A Port Huron auto worker, recently laid off during retrenchment, borrowed money from friends and neighbors, bought a small supply of whiskey, beer, and wine from contacts in Sarnia, Ontario, and converted the basement of his home into a speakeasy. He built a bar, bought second-hand tables and chairs, purchased a slot machine, and opened for business. For several months his business flourished. Neighbors and local factory workers dropped by nightly, often remaining until the early hours of the morning. The noisy behavior of patrons soon brought complaints from the neighbors, and the Port Huron police were notified. They raided the speakeasy, broke up his tables and chairs, and confiscated his slot machine and his supply of beer, gin, and whiskey hidden in the attic.[13]

Detroit also had its share of residential speakeasies located in the homes of residents and usually catering to neighborhood clients. One Detroiter recently recalled his experience as a young boy in Detroit. During one Christmas season he helped his father, a Detroit fireman, deliver Christmas gifts to the "poor people of Detroit" on behalf of the Goodfellows. The young boy was shocked to discover that many of the homes visited were also speakeasies with "tavern–like bars." His dad had so many drinks, the boy recalled, that he had to be carried home.[14]

The facilities, service, and menus of speakeasies varied greatly according to the resources of the operators, the location, and the clientele. Many speakeasies captured the atmosphere and appearance of earlier saloons and taverns. The long bar and high stools, tables with checkered cloths, and sawdust on the floor typified the decor. In fact, there was often little need to change the decor since many taverns continued to operate throughout Prohibition with facilities that had existed for several generations.

The more exclusive speakeasies operated differently. They enforced dress codes, and bouncers monitored the behavior of patrons. The Blossom Heath on East Jefferson in St. Clair Shores featured dancing nightly as well as an excellent cuisine. In May 1926 six hundred people attended the opening of the Lantern Room redecorated to represent the streets of the Montmarte district of Paris. Bouncers carefully interviewed all newcomers who entered the restaurant and monitored appropriate behavior. Liquor was readily available to trusted patrons.[15]

Many of Detroit's blind pigs offered free lunches or inexpensive meals, a tradition from taverns and saloons of an earlier period. Boiled eggs, nuts, sandwiches, and fish and chips were available for patrons who purchased one or more drinks, discouraging freeloaders from returning. Rival restaurant owners complained about the "unfair competition" of such free meals, but the police were often reluctant to act unless patrons became ill from food poisoning.[16]

Gambling was also a popular activity in many Detroit area speakeasies. Slot machines or "one–armed bandits" could be found in most well–run establishments, and in the more exclusive clubs roulette, blackjack, poker, and other games of chance flourished. The notorious Green Lantern Club in Ecorse featured blackjack games around the clock.[17] When the state police raided the Blossom Heath on July 12, 1931, they found and confiscated "one slot machine, four roulette wheels and tables, one Black Jack table, one crap table, and several hundred poker chips." They arrested the owner of the club, Danny Sullivan, and fined him one hundred dollars plus forty–five dollars in costs. Nine patrons, including several prominent local citizens, were also arrested for "frequenting a gambling place" and each was fined fifty dollars plus fifteen dollars in costs. The next month, on August 31, the state police again raided the Blossom Heath and this time confiscated "three roulette tables, one crap table, one klondike table and two thousand poker chips" and a supply of liquor.[18]

Prostitution often accompanied the activities of speakeasies, especially those establishments run by organized criminal gangs. Police and court records attest to this illicit activity associated with illegal liquor. In 1923 when Governor Alex Groesbeck sent the state police to clean up Hamtramck, they closed 150 prostitution rings, all connected to speakeasies. The state police discovered that the most popular speakeasy in town not only was located next to the city police department, but counted police officers and city officials among its steadiest customers. They also discovered that automobiles parked next to plant gates of the Hamtramck automobile factories sold liquor by the shot.[19]

The lure and attraction of the speakeasy during Prohibition is not difficult to understand, given the commonly accepted public attitude toward drinking and the minimal penalties for breaking the law. Patrons frequented these establishments for a number of reasons. Some wanted a drink with lunch or at the end of a day, the "free lunch" attracted others, and Detroit had its share of alcoholics who needed liquor daily. The thrill of engaging in an illegal activity also appealed, especially to the younger generation. Such activities provided grist for lurid accounts of visits to local speakeasies and became a status symbol to many.

The fact that visits to speakeasies could involve some danger also had its appeal. Fights and drunken brawls often erupted even in speakeasies that employed guards and bouncers. The most serious threat to patrons involved attacks by rival gangs who raided competitors or who sought to collect protection fees. One Detroit reporter observed that many former speakeasy proprietors "still had crinks in their necks from jerking their heads around to note suddenly opened doors."[20]

Police raids also concerned proprietors and other patrons. Although fines were minimal for frequenting a speakeasy or gambling place, it might be embarrassing to have one's name printed in a local newspaper. With axes and sledge hammers police destroyed tables, bars, and gambling equipment. Liquor, firearms, and slot machines were usually taken away and later dumped into the Detroit River or Lake St. Clair. Such a police practice attracted the attention of the former mayor of Detroit, Coleman Young, who as a young boy watched with very special interest the police dumping liquor into the Detroit River. He and his young friends later recovered the liquor and sold it to Little Harry's, a restaurant at Chene Street, and other speakeasies on East Jefferson Avenue.[21]

Police did not raid or close all Detroit area speakeasies, even though it was common knowledge that they were in operation. Bribery of local police officials resulted in canceled potential raids or warnings to speakeasy proprietors of impending police action. Speakeasies with unruly customers or the periodic scene of brawls and fights became key targets. Police also took food poisoning seriously. However, many speakeasy proprietors considered a police raid of little consequence, merely an inconvenience. The Blossom Heath was raided periodically, for example, and each time opened shortly afterward.[22]

One of the most famous police raids involved the Deutches Haus on Mack Avenue and Maxwell Street in Detroit. During one of many raids on the famous club, the state police and federal Prohibition authorities broke up a large party of eight hundred individuals. They discovered two bars crowded with drinking patrons and a large supply of beer and whiskey which they destroyed. The raid was typical, except for one feature. Among the patrons at the party were Detroit Mayor John Smith, Michigan Congressman Robert Clancy, and Sheriff Edward Stein. Even the Detroit Police Department was not informed of the raid in advance.[23]

The Detroit Police gave high priority to closing blind pigs located near churches and public schools. After it was discovered that young school children were encouraged to frequent speakeasies to buy liquor, a community crusade was mounted. Local police established safety zones around schools and rigidly enforced them.[24]

Area police and courts treated inebriated individuals leniently. Unless they created a public disturbance, police escorted them home or locked them up overnight for their own protection. They were allowed to go home the following morning without a fine or a court appearance. In 1927 alone twenty–three thousand such "golden rule arrests" occurred in Detroit.[25]

Accurate statistics on the number of speakeasies and blind pigs operating in the metropolitan area during Prohibition do not exist, nor can the exact number of raids by police and federal agents be determined. But from newspaper accounts and police and court records, it is clear that thousands of such illegal facilities were active during the 1920s. One reporter vividly described the consumption of alcohol in the Detroit area when he wrote, "It was absolutely impossible to get a drink in Detroit unless you walked at least ten feet and told the busy bartender what you wanted in a voice loud enough for him to hear you above the uproar."[26]

Although speakeasies provided a major supply of liquor, they were by no means the only source. Private clubs and organizations also maintained large supplies to dispense to their members at meetings and special events. The prestigious Prismatic Club of Detroit usually provided drinks for members at their weekly Saturday evening meetings. The attendance dropped when liquor was not available.

Drinking on college and university campuses in Michigan also continued during Prohibition, but did not seem to be a common problem to university and college administrators. Students, like the rest of that age group, were prone to break established rules of behavior. They were thrilled at breaking the law and they bragged about their drinking escapades and visits to local speakeasies. Nonetheless, at many of the larger universities, like the University of Michigan, most of the drinking took place in fraternities and sororities, not in local speakeasies. During the 1920s nineteen fraternities at the University of Michigan received reprimands or were closed because of liquor violations. In many instances, it was not the students that were responsible but rather alumni who returned to their fraternities, especially during football season, laden with bottles of liquor for drinking parties.[27]

Many Detroiters who were afraid of being arrested in speakeasies or who disliked the camaraderie of such places, did their drinking at home. It took a mere phone call to arrange for home delivery of a bottle or a case of liquor or a barrel of beer. In some neighborhoods nighttime deliveries prevented transactions from being observed; in most residential areas of greater Detroit, however, daytime deliveries were more common.[28] In some communities recipients even considered the delivery of liquor a status symbol. Few arrests were made. The local police devoted their attention rather to the smuggling of liquor from Canada and the home production of beer and whiskey.

Another source of liquor, of course, was that prescribed by physicians for medicinal purposes. Under the terms of the Eighteenth Amendment, liquor could be so obtained with a doctor's prescription. During the first six months of Prohibition, fifteen thousand physicians and fifty–seven thousand druggists applied for licenses to dispense liquor. By diluting the liquor druggists could dispense with large quantities illegally. In the early years of Prohibition physicians issued thousands of prescriptions and so abused the medicinal provision that the Michigan state legislature put limits on the number of prescriptions containing liquor that could be issued each month. Each issuance of a prescription containing liquor had to be filed with authorities from Lansing, and their stated purposes give us some idea of the rationale for the medicinal liquor. The majority of prescriptions were issued to aid patients in relaxing and sleeping.

Ironically, one physician advised his patient to use the liquor, "for stimulation until stimulated."[29]

The Stills

During the 1920s constant national attention was given to rumrunning across the waterway separating Ontario and Michigan. Detroit newspapers daily covered the activity, and the national media, which assigned top seasoned reporters to cover the smuggling operation in the Motor City, soon joined the local news. The colorful accounts of how liquor was smuggled across the Detroit River under the so–called watchful eyes of state and local police and the federal Prohibition Unit captured the public's interest. The violence and gang warfare associated with smuggling made daily headlines.

This deserved media attention was based solely on the astronomical volume of liquor smuggled from Canada into the Detroit area. Often overlooked, however, was the larger quantity of hard liquor, beer, and wine manufactured illegally during Prohibition within the greater Detroit area. By the mid–twenties the local output reached millions of gallons of beer and hard liquor each year and this output continued until the end of Prohibition in 1933.

Prior to Prohibition Detroit was one of the centers of beer production in the United States. With Michigan's and Detroit's heavy German populations, the industry flourished, supplying Michigan and other midwestern states with premier German beer. The passage of the Eighteenth Amendment and the Volstead Act forced most of these breweries to close or convert their facilities to other uses. Some became cold storage warehouses; others were used for manufacturing other commercial uses.

The Stroh Brewery in Detroit continued operations but on a much smaller scale. In 1918, in preparation for Prohibition, it began the production of ginger ale, other soft drinks, and ice cream—which, seventy–five years later, was still a highly acclaimed product. Of special interest was Stroh's "Hopped Malt Syrup" which went on the market in the 1920s. Its label stated: "Baking, Confections, Beverages" with a "Rich Bohemian Hop Flavor, Light or Dark." Most Detroiters knew that the syrup wasn't produced to help customers bake cakes.

The Stroh Brewery, like several others, also produced a "near beer" or "temperance beer." Under the Volstead Act it was illegal to manufacture beer containing more than one–half of one percent alcohol. Near beer had to meet these requirements. But to manufacture such legal beer, it was necessary to first produce genuine beer with an alcoholic content of from 3 to 5 percent and then remove most of the alcohol until it met the legal requirements.[30]

Near beer never caught on in the Detroit area, most likely because it was so easy to obtain genuine beer from speakeasies and bootleggers. The importance of near beer was that it allowed brewers unlimited opportunities to violate the Volstead Act. The Michigan Drug Commission and the Federal Prohibition Unit had small staffs of inspectors who could not possibly examine all of the near beer produced. Thousands of cases of genuine beer found their way to speakeasies. Furthermore, even after the beer had been examined and approved, unscrupulous brewers supplied distributors with alcohol to add to the product.

Commercial stills located in all communities of the greater Detroit area served as the major sources of illegal liquor, other than smuggled Canadian products. While no statistics exist on the exact number of such establishments in operation during Prohibition, we do know it was very substantial. In 1928 more than five thousand stills were estimated to be producing liquor in Detroit.[31] Home brewers were also busy during Prohibition, numbering in the tens of thousands. Indeed, during the period from January to July 1932, the state of Michigan's Bureau of Taxation reported that fourteen million gallons of home brew were manufactured in Detroit.[32] Adding Ecorse, Wyandotte, Hamtramck, and Port Huron, as well as other Michigan cities, to this figure increased the totals sharply.

All sections of the metropolitan Detroit area contained stills, set up in all types of buildings. Warehouses, vacant factories, and commercial structures became the sites of the large distillery operations which required not only large facilities for the stills and bottling equipment but also convenient loading docks. One major downtown Detroit still was just off Woodward Avenue, actually built in a subterranean facility, occupying a city block with "interconnecting tunnels and passageways."[33]

The operation of stills often involved danger. The threat of police raids was always a problem, even when some police were on the payroll. Federal Prohibition officers and state police often acted independently when they suspected the corruption of local police. Attacks by rival bootleggers sometimes occurred, and fires and explosions constantly threatened the operations. In the long run, however, the huge profits justified the dangers. A commercial still which could produce seventy–five to one hundred gallons of liquor a day could be purchased for five hundred dollars. Liquor costing fifty cents a gallon to produce in such a still sold on the local market for three to four dollars. A still could pay for itself in a week and soon make large profits. Within a few months of operation still operators realized substantial fortunes and, even if police raided and destroyed a still, the fines were minimal and new stills could be built within days.[34]

Home brewing and distilling grew in popularity in the Detroit area as well. Families could easily purchase equipment and supplies for a few dollars and produce enough for family and friends. Those stills were located in attics and basements of homes and garages situated in alleys at the rear of the homes. This type of bootlegging, however, could not be kept a secret from the neighbors who could observe the delivery of bags of corn sugar and detect the odor of a still. Clogged drains, fires, and explosion, as well as the arrival and departure of delivery wagons, revealed the location of neighborhood stills. If the community complained enough, local police raided the stills; if not, the stills were left alone.

Another major source of liquor production involved the use of industrial alcohol. By 1920 when Prohibition began, the chemical industry in the United States had perfected the manufacture of this product which could easily be used to produce liquor. By 1920 the production of denatured alcohol had jumped from seven million gallons in 1910 to twenty–eight million gallons. During Prohibition it became the source of millions of gallons of illicit booze. For every gallon of industrial alcohol, three gallons of liquor could be produced. Even the federal government's attempt to curb its use by forcing chemical companies to put wood alcohol and other poisons in it failed.[35]

Detroiters also used industrial alcohol in their homes. With a small supply of industrial alcohol, readily available and legal, gin could easily be produced. Distilled water was added to the raw alcohol along with a few drops of juniper juice. The bottled concoction was then shaken and rolled across the floor for ten minutes to provide "proper aging."[36]

Detroiters also produced homemade wine in large quantities. Under the Volstead Act it was legal to ferment wine for private home consumption. Local families, especially the large population of Italian Americans who had long mastered the manufacture of wine, produced tens of thousands of gallons annually. California wine growers assisted in those ventures by producing dehydrated grape bricks which were sold in local stores.

In a highly publicized case in the Upper Peninsula of Michigan the question of the legality of the homemade wine resulted in a controversy between the federal government and the state of Michigan and local residents. In February 1920 in an incident popularly called the "Iron River Rum Rebellion" state police officers raided three homes in Iron River and confiscated several barrels of "Dago Red," a popular wine among local Italian workers. The wine was promptly returned after a local state's attorney advised the police that the raid was illegal. However, several days later state police and federal Prohibition agents seized the same wine. After some

81

hours of heated arguments between the police and state's attorneys causing great community tension, the matter was resolved. The resulting ruling stated that the police did not have the required warrants and that home production and consumption of wine did not violate the Volstead Act.[37]

Rumrunners shared the Detroit River with thousands of excursion vessels, tankers, ore carriers, and pleasure craft. The Detroit skyline is seen here from downtown Windsor in the 1920s. Courtesy: Dossin Great Lakes Museum.

A *Detroit News* helicopter over downtown Detroit. Courtesy: Dossin Great Lakes Museum.

Cadillac Square, Detroit. Courtesy: Dossin Great Lakes Museum.

Woodward at Michigan Avenue, Detroit, in 1922. Courtesy: Burton Historical Collection.

Dozens of speakeasies operated near Cadillac Square, Detroit, throughout Prohibition.
Courtesy: Burton Historical Collection.

Stroh's Ginger Ale is advertised at 729 Woodward, Detroit. The company also produced ice cream and temperance beer. Courtesy: Burton Historical Collection.

Cadillac Square, Detroit, 1920s. Courtesy: Burton Historical Collection.

Changing shifts at the Ford Plant in Highland Park. Shots of liquor could be purchased
from parked cars near auto plants for twenty cents. Courtesy: Burton Historical Collection.

Woodward Avenue at Seven Mile Road, Detroit, in September 1927. Speakeasies were
located along Woodward Avenue and outlying suburbs serving commuters as well as local
citizens. Courtesy: Burton Historical Collection.

Riverside Park at East Jefferson Avenue and the Belle Isle Bridge.
Courtesy: Burton Historical Collection.

Detroit was the center of boat races and the manufacturing of boat engines. Many of
the powerful boats were also used in smuggling, easily outrunning police patrol boats.
Courtesy: Dossin Great Lakes Museum.

Belle Isle, Detroit's most popular recreational area in the 1920s, was less than a mile from the Canadian side of the Detroit River. Hundreds of rumrunners crossed here and unloaded their cargoes to waiting automobiles. This scene is of a Spanish American War Veterans' Picnic on August 29, 1927. Tailgate parties featuring beer and whiskey were popular. Courtesy: Dossin Great Lakes Museum.

Hundreds of docks, boat slips, and boat canals lined the Detroit River from Toledo to Port Huron. They were a haven for rumrunners seeking shelter from patrol boats. Courtesy: Dossin Great Lakes Museum.

The dock at Sarnia, Ontario, was also active in the liquor traffic between Ontario and Michigan, although not as busy as the Detroit River. The St. Clair River was also used extensively by rumrunners. Courtesy: Dossin Great Lakes Museum.

The Flapper Girl of the 1920s. Courtesy: Library of Congress.

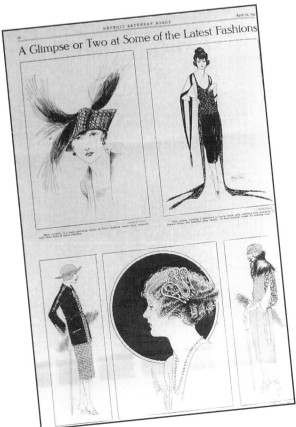

The Prohibition years witnessed the emergence of the new fashions for women and men. The popular newspaper, the *Detroit Saturday Night*, devoted hundreds of pages to these fashions. Courtesy: Burton Historical Collection.

Grosse Pointers in the style of the 1920s in a new Ford sedan.
Courtesy: Library of Congress.

Flappers demonstrate the latest in cigarette holders, 1924.
Courtesy: Library of Congress.

Palais de Danse
Jefferson and Sheridan

With its Famous Orchestra, Splendid Floor and Beautiful Surroundings is Preferred by Particular People. Dancing Every Evening

Dances and dancing marathons were crazes of the 1920s in Detroit. Bootleg liquor was usually available if you carried a hip flask or parked your car near the dance hall. Courtesy: Burton Historical Collection.

Detroiters in the 1920s welcomed WWJ and the beginning of regularly scheduled radio programs, *Life Magazine*, September 27, 1927. Courtesy: Library of Congress.

"A girl who sips ice water is looked upon as freezing the party" from Harper's *Bazaar*, June 1928. Courtesy: Library of Congress.

During the 1926 Detroit Chamber of Commerce cruise, the SS *Noronic* was raided by federal agents who discovered several hundred cases of beer and whiskey. Chamber officials denied any knowledge of the liquor and couldn't explain how it got there. Courtesy: Dossin Great Lakes Museum.

Thousands of pedestrians and clogged city streets were typical of downtown Detroit during Prohibition. Michigan Avenue at noon in front of the Book Cadillac Hotel. Courtesy: Burton Historical Collection.

Speakeasies were located along this stretch of Woodward Avenue (looking north from State Street), October 29, 1929. Courtesy: *Detroit Free Press.*

Bustling downtown Detroit at Broadway in the 1920s. Courtesy: Burton Historical Collection.

Guest cards were given to trusted patrons by Detroit area speakeasies.
Courtesy: Detroit Historical Museum.

A blind pig at 8756 Linwood Avenue occupied two store spaces. It was raided by police on July 22, 1932. A large quantity of liquor was confiscated, the barkeeper arrested, and furnishings and equipment destroyed. Courtesy: *Detroit News.*

Despite the widespread violation of liquor laws, there was strong opposition to the location of blind pigs near schools or churches. This blind pig located near the Craft Public School on Michigan Avenue was raided on April 19, 1930, after numerous complaints from neighbors and civic groups. Courtesy: *Detroit News.*

This blind pig, located near the Wesley Methodist Church on Grand River Avenue, Detroit, was raided by police on April 19, 1930. Courtesy: *Detroit News.*

With the advent of Prohibition, Stroh's and other breweries produced temperance or near beer with an alcoholic content of less than .5 percent. Courtesy: Stroh Archives.

A well–stocked bar, slot machines, and spittoons catered to daily patrons at the speakeasy at 86 Gratiot Avenue. Courtesy: Burton Historical Collection.

Windsor, Ontario, also had its share of speakeasies. Checkered tablecloths and saw-dust on floors were popular. Courtesy: *Windsor Star.*

From the looks on their faces these Windsorites were enjoy-ing their evening at a Windsor speakeasy. Courtesy: *Windsor Star.*

BEVERAGE LIST

	PINTS
White Rock Water	80
Appolinaris Water	85
Royal Ross Soda Water	80
White Rock Ginger Ale	85
Canada Dry Ginger Ale	90
A & B Ginger Ale	80

BOTTLED BEER

Budweiser	50
Strohs	50
New Berghoff's Special XX Beer	50

MENU

Canape, Moscovite
———
Celery   Olives
———
Clear Turtle in Cup
———
Salted Almonds
———
Roast Whole Squab Chicken, Wolverine
Parisian Potatoes
———
California Asparagus, Vinaigrette
———
Nesselrode Pudding
———
Petite Four
———
Coffee

The Hotel Wolverine served beer at its
New Year's Eve celebration in 1926.
Courtesy: Dossin Great Lakes Museum.

HOTEL WOLVERINE
ELIZABETH STREET EAST
AT WOODWARD AVE.
DETROIT

A Happy New Year
1926

DECEMBER 31, 1925-1926

East side, west side,
All around the block,
The Bootlegger's
rushin' bizness
At all hours
of the clock.

Beer and whiskey were readily
available in most every town in
Michigan. Detroit residents could
purchase supplies at local
speakeasies or have it delivered to
their homes. This cartoon reflected
the ease of securing such contraband liquor. Courtesy: Dossin Great
Lakes Museum.

4

ENFORCEMENT OF THE VOLSTEAD ACT

THE PROHIBITION NAVY

THE PROVISIONS OF the Volstead Act divided the enforcement of the Eighteenth Amendment among the federal, state, and local units of government. On the federal level the United States Customs Service under the Department of Treasury, the U.S. Coast Guard, a specially established Prohibition Unit, and other divisions of the Bureau of Internal Revenue had responsibility for enforcing the law. The state police of Michigan, the state Food and Drug Department, and the police departments of Michigan towns and cities shared responsibilities for curbing smuggling and the illegal operation of speakeasies and stills.

Michigan officials, who had already spent two years fighting smuggling from wet Ohio into dry Michigan, were aware from the beginning of the problems they faced in trying to control the border along the waterway that separated Michigan and Ontario. The United States Congress and the executive branch of the federal government, on the other hand, were totally unprepared for the magnitude of the enforcement problems which faced them. After all, the Eighteenth Amendment was passed easily by huge margins throughout the United States. The widespread public support for Prohibition, they assumed, would be a major factor in marshalling like support for enforcement. As a result of this misguided view, Congress provided only meager resources for controlling smuggling and other violations of the Volstead Act.[1]

Congressional leaders also miscalculated by assuming that Canada would pass similar legislation banning the manufacture, sale, exportation, and consumption of liquor and other alcoholic beverages. After all, the movement for Prohibition had been strong throughout Canada, and every province except Quebec had outlawed the sale of liquor. Within months after the Volstead Act went into effect, however, American leaders recognized their mistake. The Canadian government in Ottawa had not embraced Prohibition; its official position was one of "non interference" and "non cooperation." As a result, the total burden of enforcing Prohibition rested solely upon federal, state, and local agencies in the United States.[2]

Congress's underestimation of the difficulty of enforcing Prohibition soon proved costly. The magnitude of smuggling activity overwhelmed existing customs and police agencies were overwhelmed by the magnitude of smuggling. As one historian described the situation, "Before the Coast Guard knew what had happened, it found itself in a futile stern chase." State and local police officials throughout Michigan expressed the same sentiment.[3]

Federal, state, and local agencies also

lacked a coordinated effort, a major problem which plagued enforcement efforts for the thirteen years of Prohibition. At first, there was practically no coordination even among the U.S. Customs Patrol, the federal Prohibition Unit, and the U.S. Coast Guard. Finally, in 1926 all federal enforcement programs were placed under the command of the U.S. Collector of Customs in Detroit who established a coordinated effort. The Prohibition enforcement program of the Michigan State Police and local police agencies also lacked coordination. The extensive collusion between enforcement officers and smugglers further compromised successful law enforcement.

Smuggling on the waterway between Ontario and Michigan, especially the Detroit River and Lake St. Clair, needed to be stopped. But the limited size of the staff and the length of the water-way—some four hundred miles from Lake Erie to Lake Superior—made the task formidable, and the financial resources and modern equipment of smugglers made the struggle nearly impossible. From the beginning rumrunners availed themselves of hundreds of powerful river boats, which could easily outrun and outdistance the vessels used by state and Detroit police agencies. In 1920 the Detroit Police Department, responsible for the major smuggling avenue across the Detroit River, had only one patrol boat which, according to Detroit Police Commissioner James Inches, was "a good seaworthy scow that by an effort could overhaul a tug boat." Rumrunners were "running circles around us," he complained.[4]

As the smuggling crisis heightened late in 1920, the mayor and the City Council of Detroit recognized the need for additional staff and patrol boats. In 1921 the Detroit Police Department commissioned two new patrol boats for service on the Detroit River. Later in the year in August, the Michigan State Police announced its presence in the Detroit area with its own river patrol, "a single ancient craft" armed with machine guns and rifles to slow down escaping rumrunners. The following year the state police commissioned several new powerful river craft with two hundred horse power engines, capable of speeds of thirty–eight miles an hour, to patrol the Detroit River and Lake St. Clair. In addition to these police vessels, other river craft captured from rumrunners were recommissioned and used to augment the police river patrol. In 1920 Detroit police captured the *Tennessee II,* a large and powerful vessel, while rumrunners unloaded its contraband cargo of Canadian whiskey. It, too, became part of the police patrol fleet.[5]

The U.S. Coast Guard also increased its presence on the Michigan–Ontario waterway in the mid–1920s. When Prohibition went into effect, the Coast Guard assigned most of its vessels to patrol along the East Coast, especially near the major ports. Thousands of ocean vessels, laden with liquor and with foreign registry for protection against seizure by the Coast Guard, anchored themselves beyond the three–mile limit in international waters. They waited there for coastal boats, usually under the cover of darkness, to come out to purchase cases of liquor and then try to evade capture by the Coast Guard on their return to port on the mainland. "Rum Row," as the off–shore strip of international waters was popularly called, continued to receive the major attention of the Coast Guard until the mid–1920s when they finally recognized that the Great Lakes, and especially the Michigan–Ontario waterway, had become the main avenue of smuggling.

Because of their size, most of the U.S. Coast Guard vessels were assigned duty on Lake Erie, the Detroit River as far north as Grosse Ile, and then north of Marine City on the St. Clair River. The smaller craft of the Michigan and Detroit police, as well as the U.S. Customs and other federal agencies, were assigned duty on the Detroit River north of Grosse Ile, Lake St. Clair, and the St. Clair River. The press covering rumrunning for local and major newspapers and journals observed the strange assortment of vessels, under different commands, flying different insignias, and manned by men with different uniforms, and dubbed the vessels the "Prohibition Navy."

Despite the number of enforcement vessels and their practice to race up and down the Detroit River during daylight hours, they still could not match the powerful, well-organized rumrunners who controlled the waterway. Each year several million cases of smuggled Canadian liquor arrived into metropolitan Detroit, and despite the increasing number of arrests, the flow of whiskey continued uninterrupted. In 1928, according to federal sources, only 5 percent of the liquor leaving the Ontario export docks along the Detroit River were seized. Most of the remaining 95 percent ended up in the United States.[6]

A shortage of Prohibition enforcement vessels and staff and a lack of coordination among federal, state, and local authorities hindered successful intervention. To make matters even worse, a sharp competition existed among the three groups. Each had its own leaders, agenda, and priorities. They often blamed each other in the media for failure to enforce the Volstead Act.

Disposing of the thousands of boats and automobiles seized in raids of rumrunners also created problems for enforcement officials. Confiscated boats, for example, were often purchased at auction for ridiculously low prices by the very smugglers who had owned them previously. Frequently the same boat was seized several times a year from the same smuggler. In other cases confiscated boats and automobiles disappeared from police custody before the scheduled auction. In April 1929, 360 boats seized from

rumrunners, valued at $15,000, disappeared from a U.S. Border Patrol marina in Lake St. Clair near Selfridge Air Field. No official explanation was ever given, but within days many of the boats were again engaged in smuggling.[7]

The difficulty of recruiting competent and trained agents to work for the Prohibition Navy posed a serious problem. Low morale and low pay—less than two thousand dollars a year—added to the problem of recruitment. As a result, most of the new employees, assigned to the waterway patrols, had no experience in operating boats or handling firearms. Numerous accidents occurred because of the actions of inexperienced seamen. Collisions were all too common, and many patrol boats were damaged by chasing rumrunners in shallow water. Overzealous patrol agents sometimes mistook innocent pleasure boaters and fishermen for smugglers. This was especially true of patrol boats armed with machine guns, rifles, and other weapons. In 1925 federal agents fired upon two sons of prominent Detroit business leaders when they failed to stop their boat. The boys had misunderstood the signal to stop and continued on their sightseeing journey. Their boat was hit several times by rifle fire and the boys narrowly escaped being hit. In another highly publicized incident, a federal patrol boat in pursuit of a rumrunner rammed a pleasure boat, killing a Detroit resident and his eleven-year-old daughter.[8]

Federal agents also incurred the wrath and criticism of wealthy Detroit and Grosse Pointe residents who lived along the Detroit River and Lake St. Clair. In search for rumrunners, they often broke into the boathouses along the water. On several occasions, the boathouse of Henry B. Joy, the prominent automobile manufacturer and Grosse Pointe civic leader, was the target. Joy was so incensed by the raids, the damage inflicted upon his property, and the treatment of his family and staff that he took his complaint to his friend, Andrew Mellon, the U.S. secretary of the treasury. In a decision directly related to those incidents, Henry Joy became a national spokesman in the campaign to repeal the Eighteenth Amendment.[9]

Many customs and Prohibition agents, as well as police, were on the payroll of smugglers. For the standard payment of five hundred dollars, enforcement officers called in sick, allowing hundreds of shipments to cross the Detroit River without detection. Some even more helpful police protected smugglers who crossed the river, unloaded their cargoes, and delivered liquor to local speakeasies. The crew of the U.S. Coast Guard cutter 219, operating out of Monroe, Michigan, was apprehended in 1929 and convicted after they had seized a boatload of contraband Canadian whiskey and transferred it to another rumrunning vessel.[10] Between 1920 and 1926 a total of 750 Coast Guard employees were dismissed of "misconduct and delinquency," and during the

following two years an additional 550 Coast Guard men were charged with "extortion, bribery, solicitation of money, illegal disposition of liquor, and making false reports of theft."[11]

The U.S. Customs Patrol faced similar charges of bribery and graft. In December 1928 the *New York Times* reported that from fifty to one hundred customs officers had been indicted and convicted on corruption and bribery charges involving the smuggling of liquor.[12] Local police officers in Detroit and other metropolitan communities were faced with similar charges. In April 1929, for example, the Detroit harbormaster and commanding officer of the Belle Isle police station was suspended for his role in smuggling. He had not only used police patrol boats to escort rumrunners across the Detroit River and Lake St. Clair, but he also allowed smugglers to store contraband Canadian whiskey in his quarters on Belle Isle.[13]

Honest police and customs officers also became victims of smuggling. Feuds erupted in several police departments between officers who wanted strict enforcement of the liquor laws and those who were receiving bribe money. In Wayne County such a feud ended in violence when three officers were arrested for the murder of a fellow officer who had caught them in a smuggling operation. Several police officers requested transfers or other assignments because of their knowledge of corruption within the police force and their fear of reprisal.[14]

Of course, many honest and dedicated local police officers and federal Prohibition officers worked tirelessly to enforce federal and state liquor laws. One of these loyal officers was Howard Blakemore, who served as chief inspector of the U.S. Immigration Service Border Patrol from 1927 to 1941. During his career he received many threats from smugglers and dishonest enforcement officers who warned him that he would be "eliminated if he didn't lay off."[15]

With headquarters in Marine City, Michigan, Blakemore's jurisdiction included the waterway from Detroit to Harbor Beach. It was an uphill battle to patrol this long stretch of water between Ontario and Michigan. He was understaffed and without a sufficient number of patrol boats for the territory in his jurisdiction. Customs agents had to rely upon "junk cars," he complained bitterly to his superiors, which couldn't catch the "slick, new Model A Fords of the rumrunners." Despite these obstacles, Inspector Blakemore was successful in apprehending more than two hundred bootleggers between 1927 and 1933. In his memoirs he observed, "I always figured I had most of my success because I was patient. I'd lay on the beach for five hours if it was necessary." He also "crept across the frozen Lake St. Clair at night if there was a chance of collaring a rumrunner."[16]

Inspector Blakemore also later admitted that he had made mistakes in enforcing the Volstead Act. On August 1, 1928, Blakemore captured smugglers off the shore of Lexington, Michigan, in a boat laden with twenty–four hundred bottles of beer. He had two choices to consider —either to locate a truck and have the beer transported to headquarters at Marine City or dispose of the beer by dumping it into the river. He chose the latter course of action but decided not to break the bottles—as was the usual practice—because the broken glass might injure the local swimmers. He took the advice of a local Lexington, Michigan, resident who told Blakemore that the St. Clair River was more than fifteen feet deep at the end of the dock and that the strong river current would carry the beer downstream. Actually, the depth of the river at the dock's end was only six feet and there was no current. On the following day, the "Great Lexington Beer Party"—as dubbed by news reporters—took place. Villagers donned bathing suits and "everyone who could swim was tumbling off the dock in a grand and glorious scramble." When they recovered most of the beer, the "dripping divers formed a long procession as they paraded toward the town's central square, carrying cases and bottles of brew in a hedonistic display of defiance." A Port Huron news reporter described the drinking spree of the three hundred residents of Lexington who took part or watched. Blakemore's philosophical and honest response to news of the beer party was, "I was just too gullible." He later recalled, "I never heard any more of the Lexington Beer Party."[17]

Other Prohibition agents suffered greater losses than Inspector Blakemore. Many were injured or lost their lives while on duty—in boating accidents and while apprehending rumrunners. Earl Roberts, a new recruit to the U.S. Customs Border Patrol, was shot in March 1929 as he boarded a rumrunner's boat crossing the St. Clair River between Port Lambton, Ontario, and Algonac, Michigan. He died the following day of gunshot wounds. His assistant was convicted and spent nineteen years in prison.[18] Between January 16, 1920, and October 31, 1927, forty–seven U.S. Prohibition officers were killed in the line of duty enforcing the Volstead Act.[19]

The Detroit River and the rest of the long waterway to Sault Ste. Marie was a dangerous place to be as long as smuggling was such a profitable business. But after 1923, when organized criminal gangs on both sides of the river had taken over control of smuggling and the operation of commercial stills and speakeasies, violence and violations of the law increased sharply. With unlimited resources these gangs were not only able to purchase powerful boats and hire armed crews to run them, but they were able to place hundreds of law enforcement employees on their payroll. They made millions from the sale of illegal liquor.

Numerous gangs operated on the Detroit River and Lake St. Clair, more or less dividing the waterway into sections, each under the control of one organized criminal group or combine. Of these, the Purple Gang was most notorious and powerful. Made up of several young Jewish hoodlums who grew up together on the east side, they turned their attention to smuggling after they had merged with the Oakland Sugar House Gang. They manufactured and distributed bootleg liquor and beer, they smuggled choice Canadian whiskey from Canada, and they controlled many Detroit area speakeasies. For years, the Purple Gang was the major supplier for Al Capone and his Chicago criminal empire. They met his demand for hundreds of thousands of cases of Old Log Cabin Whiskey, which was shipped to Chicago by truck and railroad. The influence of the Purple Gang declined sharply in 1929 after the arrest and conviction of several of its leaders and the murder of other gang members.[20]

Also active in the 1920s were several Italian Mafia gangs— led by the Licavoli, Vitalie, and Giannolos families. They not only had extensive smuggling operations in the Detroit area, including breweries and speakeasies, but they acquired controlling interest in several Canadian distilleries and breweries. The competing gangs divided up the waterway, and if one gang infringed on another's designated section, open warfare, murder, and hijacking followed. Unfortunately, many innocent pleasure boaters and fishermen fell victim to the violence.

Federal and state enforcement agencies organized campaigns against the gangs but experienced only temporary success. The gangs' unlimited financial resources assembled from the astronomical profits from smuggling enabled them to not only successfully bribe liquor enforcement officials, but also take control of some local governments. In Hamtramck, Ecorse, and Wyandotte in the 1920s the gangs had key city officials on their payrolls, and in all of the communities rumrunning, stills, speakeasies, and gambling flourished.

Ecorse, a small community on the Detroit River, ten miles from downtown Detroit, vied with Hamtramck for the reputation as the most corrupt community in the state. Located opposite Grosse Ile and several Canadian export docks, Ecorse saw a steady flow of liquor come into its harbor. Marinas and boat slips and houses lined the shore, providing ideal facilities for hurriedly unloading contraband liquor. Hundreds of local residents, eager for quick profits, got involved in smuggling from the opening day of Prohibition. Local fishermen converted their crafts to store cases of liquor rather than fish. With initial profits, they purchased larger and more expensive boats. Even tug boats were acquired and put in the liquor trade, often dragging scows and rafts filled with sacks of whiskey.[21]

During cold winter months when ice covered the Detroit River, Ecorse citizens purchased cheap jalopies and removed doors for quick escape in case they sank through thin ice. Thousands of cases of Canadian whiskey arrived in Ecorse each month, some earmarked for local speakeasies like Lefty Clark's Dice Parlor and the Green Lantern, "Where a lively blackjack game ran around the clock." Most of the liquor was shipped to Chicago and other midwestern cities.

The Ecorse liquor operation, however, was not limited to a few enterprising citizens or gangsters. Pervasive smuggling encompassed all segments of the community. According to a prominent Ecorse resident interviewed in 1921, "Ninety percent of Ecorsians were at the present writing our bootleggers, and the remaining ten percent were patented bootleggers, too old or infirm to give a hand in carrying a box."[22] Smuggling involved men and women of all ages and whole families. High school students, ages thirteen to sixteen, were hired to deliver liquor from boats to road houses.

Federal and state officials were fully aware of the widespread smuggling activities in Ecorse, but there were limits to curbing the trade. The large number of boathouses along the river front, many with tunnels to houses several hundred feet away, made it easy to hide contraband liquor. Furthermore, most elected public officials and members of the local police department either sympathized with the smugglers or joined the operation and were put on the payroll of the bootleggers and other gangs. They notified smugglers of impending state police or border patrol raids and refused to cooperate in curbing the illicit liquor trade. On one occasion, a large group of Ecorse citizens tried to block the Border Patrol from confiscating the boats of smugglers at a local dock. One reporter for the *Literary Digest* referred to Ecorse as "that amazing nest of smugglers, in which even large armed squads of American enforcement officers feel uncomfortable. . . ." [23]

The appeal of smuggling Canadian whiskey and beer influenced the residents of Hamtramck, another Detroit area city. Located within the boundaries of Detroit, it was in 1920 one of Michigan's largest cities, consisting of fifty thousand residents, most of whom were Polish immigrants who were "distrustful of and rebellious against American laws."[24] Hamtramck residents intensely disliked and violated the Eighteenth Amendment and the Volstead Act. U.S. District Judge Arthur Tuttle characterized Hamtramck as "a disreputable city, a cancer spot and a disgrace."[25]

By 1923 the situation became so bad that Governor Alex Groesbeck ordered the Michigan State Police to take over the city and conduct a thorough investigation of criminal activities there. The state police found clear proof of the extent of corruption, revealing widespread violations of the Volstead Act. They found, for example, four hundred soft drink parlors licensed by the city, serving "everything but soft drinks." Liquor was sold openly in candy and party stores, restaurants, and pool rooms. Whiskey was sold by the shot from parked automobiles outside of automobile plants and on the streets of the city.[26]

State police, during raids in 1923, seized seventy–five stills, closed two breweries, and destroyed twenty thousand gallons of moonshine liquor, along with one hundred thousand gallons of mash. They confiscated hundreds of barrels of beer and wine. The "soft drink parlors," two hundred blind pigs, one hundred fifty houses of prostitution, and numerous gambling places were also raided and put out of business.

The Michigan State Police also investigated the corruption of local public officials in Hamtramck and brought charges against many. The mayor and thirty–one other defendants, including the commissioner of public safety and a high–ranking police officer, were convicted of violating prohibition laws. Federal and state law enforcement officials applauded Governor Groesbeck for his aggressive stand against Hamtramck.[27]

Although few other Michigan communities matched the corruption of Ecorse and Hamtramck, violations of the Volstead Act were extensive. Detroit police raided and destroyed more than a thousand breweries during Prohibition. Liquor enforcement officers targeted speakeasies and blind pigs, and during the 1920s thousands of these popular watering holes were raided, closed, and padlocked. During 1928 alone, federal prosecutors started more than fifty thousand criminal prosecutions for violations of the Volstead Act, and they won 48,820 convictions.

Prohibition enforcement by the Detroit police was much less impressive. From 1918, when state Prohibition became effective, to 1928, Detroit police officers arrested 34,167 for liquor violations. Of these they won convictions for 8,864, an average of about 25 percent. From May 27, 1925, when the Michigan "Nuisance and Abatement Act" became effective, to May 1, 1928, Detroit police closed or padlocked 272 blind pigs. Local police arrested nearly ninety thousand local citizens for drunkenness between 1918 and 1928 and apprehended an additional thirty thousand as Golden Rule drunks.[28]

As the Roaring Twenties came to a close, it was obvious to the public officials and citizens alike that Prohibition in Michigan had failed. Despite the publicity given to the work of the Prohibition Navy and other federal, state, and local enforcement agencies and the continuous number of arrests and convictions in the U.S. District Court, Michigan residents, especially those who lived along the Detroit River and the rest of the Ontario–Michigan waterway, saw that smuggling continued unabated. Liquor of all varieties was readily available in all sections of the city and the rest of the state. The failure to enforce the Volstead Act also resulted in a dramatic change in public opinion regarding Prohibition. Influential civic, religious, and community leaders not only voiced concerns about enforcement practices but began to support attempts to amend the Volstead Act and even support repeal of the Eighteenth Amendment.

Thirty U.S. Border Patrol boats near the Ambassador Bridge began their summer watch of the Detroit River on April, 16, 1932. Courtesy: *Windsor Star.*

The Detroit Police patrolled the Detroit River between Windsor and Detroit. Courtesy: Burton Historical Collection.

U.S. Customs Border Patrol on duty on the Detroit River, June 26, 1929. Despite the efforts of federal and local patrols, only an estimated 5 percent of smuggled liquor was seized. Courtesy: The Press Collection, Cleveland State University.

Detroit Police at river patrol headquarters at the foot of Riopelle Street ready for patrol,
April 20, 1932. Courtesy: *Detroit News.*

Two Coast Guard patrol boats at Trenton, opposite Grosse Ile.
Courtesy: Dossin Great Lakes Museum.

Federal, state, and local liquor enforcement agencies authorized firearms and other weapons to combat rumrunners. The crew of Coast Guard cutter 236 is receiving training in the use of its one–pounder. Courtesy: Dossin Great Lakes Museum, The Press Collection, Cleveland State University.

The crew of a Coast Guard cutter unloading confiscated whiskey at Trenton, November 20, 1929. Courtesy: The Press Collection, Cleveland State University.

The St. Mary's River, connecting Lakes Huron and Superior, was another favorite crossing for rumrunners. A Coast Guard vessel is unloading a cargo of confiscated whiskey at Sault Ste. Marie. Courtesy: The Press Collection, Cleveland State University.

The Defoe Shipyard in Bay City in 1924 was under contract to build several Coast Guard cutters for duty on the Michigan–Ontario waterway. Courtesy: Institute for Great Lakes Research.

The U.S. Coast Guard Cutter *Morrill* was one of the largest patrol boats on the Michigan–Ontario waterway. Courtesy: Dossin Great Lakes Museum.

The attacks on fishing vessels and pleasure craft by federal agents caused many influential Detroiters to support revisions in the Volstead Act. Newspaper cartoons reflected changes in public attitudes toward Prohibition. Courtesy: Dossin Great Lakes Museum.

U.S. Customs agent inspecting a rumrunner captured on the Pine River, October 21, 1931. It was abandoned when capture was imminent. Courtesy: Gene Buel.

The notorious S.S. *Vedas* carried huge cargoes of Canadian beer and whiskey from Quebec to Ontario, dropping her cargo to rumrunners enroute, especially on the Detroit River. She was seized by Canadian Customs and towed to a Windsor wharf. Courtesy: *Windsor Star*.

U.S. Coast Guard seizing rumrunner, October 10, 1925. Courtesy: The Press Collection, Cleveland State University.

"A day's work!" U.S. Coast Guard agents with three rumrunners captured on the Detroit River, August 27, 1929. Courtesy: *Detroit News.*

U.S. Coast Guard cutter 216 with a seized cargo of Canadian whiskey, December 28, 1931. Courtesy: The Press Collection, Cleveland State University.

U.S. Coast Guard agents guard seized a rumrunner and large shipment of whiskey. Courtesy: Dossin Great Lakes Museum.

Detroit Police unloading whiskey seized from rumrunners on the Detroit River. Canvas sacks were used not only to carry liquor but to facilitate the recovery of liquor with grappling hooks. Courtesy: C. H. Gervais.

Beer "lugger" seized at mouth of Detroit River, July 6, 1929, by U.S. Coast Guard moored at foot of Orleans Street. Courtesy: *Detroit News.*

A typical load of Canadian liquor seized July 6, 1929. Courtesy: *Detroit News.*

Local citizens watch U.S. Customs agents inspect a seized rumrunner at Marine City, 1924. Courtesy: Gene Buel.

Federal Prohibition agents checking cache of Canadian beer, produced at the Riverside Brewery in Ontario. Courtesy: *Detroit Free Press.*

A seized cargo of Golden Wedding Canadian whiskey, June 15, 1929. Courtesy: *Detroit News.*

U.S. Customs agents unloading barrels of Canadian beer from captured boat, September 3, 1931. Courtesy: *Detroit News.*

Ontario Export Dock no. 4 on Windsor waterfront. Courtesy: *Windsor Star.*

Confiscated rumrunner autos at the U.S. Customs Border Patrol headquarters in Marine City, Michigan. Courtesy: Gene Buel.

The U.S. government auctioned captured rumrunners at the foot of Orleans Street, December 16, 1929. Many were back in action as rumrunners within days after the auction. Courtesy: *Detroit News.*

Coast Guard crew dumping seized liquor into the Detroit River. Bottles were often broken to prevent recovery. Courtesy: The Press Collection, Cleveland State University.

Deputy Marshall William "Scotty" Monteith destroying 1,000 bottles of confiscated whiskey at the foot of Orleans Street. Courtesy: *Detroit News*.

U.S. Coast Guard agent inspecting cache of confiscated Glenmore whiskey, November 22, 1922. Courtesy: Dossin Great Lakes Museum.

Most confiscated liquor was dumped into the Detroit River and Lake St. Clair. Courtesy: *Windsor Star.*

Detroit Police dumping confiscated liquor into the Detroit River off Riopelle Street. Courtesy: *Detroit News.*

130

In 1922, Detroit became the first city in the United States to use a police broadcasting system. Police cars were equipped with radios to receive messages and intercept rumrunners at landing sites. Courtesy: Archives of Labor and Urban Affairs.

A new Detroit Police patrol wagon assigned to monitor speakeasies. Courtesy: Bentley Library.

The police of St. Clair Shores patrolled Lake St. Clair as well as the shoreline. During Prohibition they arrested hundreds of rumrunners and speakeasy operators. Courtesy: Dossin Great Lakes Museum.

To combat rumrunners during winter, the Grosse Pointe Police manned ice boats on Lake St. Clair. Courtesy: National Archives.

The Licavoli Squad, led by brothers Pete and Jonnie, were rivals to the Purple Gang for control of rumrunning on the Detroit River. They dominated smuggling on the upper Detroit River, and murdered rivals, local police, and federal agents. They supplied Al Capone with tens of thousands of cases of expensive Old Log Cabin Canadian whiskey. One of their shipments to Chicago, hijacked by the Bugs Moran gang, led to the St. Valentine's Day Massacre in 1929. They are seen here in their hideout, posing with a *Toledo Blade* reporter (with hat). Courtesy: Toledo–Lucas County Public Library.

The Chicago gangster Al Capone was seen often in Detroit in the 1920s arranging for the shipment of Canadian Old Log Cabin to Chicago. Courtesy: *Windsor Star.*

U.S. Customs agents tallying liquor shipments from Ontario liquor export docks. Courtesy: The Press Collection, Cleveland State University.

Load of whiskey seized on Lonyo Road, Detroit, June 5, 1932. Courtesy: *Detroit News.*

The Purple Gang photographed in a Detroit Police lineup, March 30, 1928. By 1933 most of these men were in jail or had been murdered by rivals. Courtesy: *Detroit News.*

U.S. Custom agents checking autos at the Detroit–Windsor Tunnel.
Courtesy: Dossin Great Lakes Museum.

U.S. Customs agents impounding a rumrunner's auto at the 13th Street ferry dock.
Courtesy: Dossin Great Lakes Museum.

Detroit Police are arresting patrons of a blind pig in the Pioneer Club at 2951 East Jefferson, March 4, 1932. Courtesy: *Detroit News.*

A blind pig at 917 Farmer Street, Detroit, is padlocked by a Detroit Police official, June 1924. Courtesy: *Detroit News.*

Booze pouring out third floor windows during raid on a Gratiot Avenue still. Courtesy: *Detroit News.*

Detroit Police inspecting a large commercial still. Courtesy: *Detroit Times.*

When located and raided, stills were destroyed by authorities.
Courtesy: The Press Collection, Cleveland State University.

Results of a state police raid on a Detroit speakeasy. Courtesy: Michigan State Archives.

Police raid on a Detroit speakeasy. Apparatus for distilling liquor was also confiscated.
Courtesy: *Detroit News.*

Stroh and Tivoli beer and Canadian whiskey were confiscated in a raid by Detroit
Police. Courtesy: *Detroit News.*

Highland Park Police officers inspecting liquor seized in a raid on a speakeasy. Courtesy: *Detroit Free Press.*

Detroit Police unloading truck load of Tecumseh beer. Courtesy: *Windsor Star.*

The Oasis Club blind pig, located near the Detroit City College campus, was popular with college students. Four officers of the Canfield Police Station are behind the bar after a raid on November 30, 1932. It was reopened soon afterward. Courtesy: *Detroit News.*

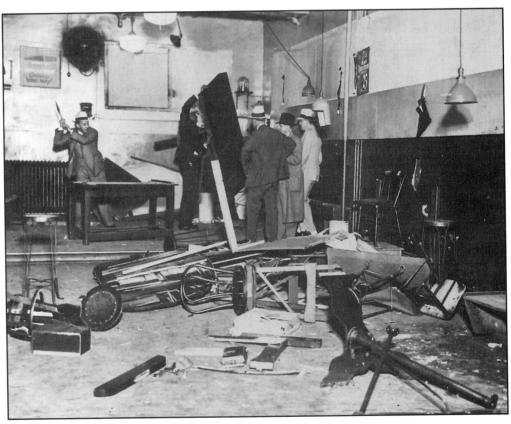

Police and Border Patrol agents destroyed this speakeasy at 2942 Woodward Avenue, September 13, 1933. Courtesy: *Detroit Free Press.*

REPEAL OF PROHIBITION
THE END OF A NOBLE EXPERIMENT

ISTORIANS OF THE Roaring Twenties have devoted special attention to the passage of the Eighteenth Amendment and the general failure of federal, state, and local police agencies to enforce the Volstead Act. Frederick Lewis Allen in *Only Yesterday* described the profound revolution in the "manners and morals" of Americans as the nation returned to "normalcy" after World War I. He carefully documented how the young "flapper" generation, with its new dress codes, fads, and almost complete disregard for the liquor laws helped defeat Prohibition. The powerful influence of ethnic groups, especially the large German population in Michigan, for whom beer, wine, and other alcoholic beverages were part of their cultural tradi-

tions, has also been researched. Michigan's large force of automobile and other factory workers who found after–shift drinks a pleasant respite from long hours in plants urged changes in liquor laws, especially the return of genuine beer. Prohibition did not alter the drinking patterns of the well–to–do Michigan residents. Cocktail parties and before–dinner drinking continued to be popular, unaffected by the remote possibility of arrest. For millions of Americans Prohibition brought few changes in drinking habits. The passage of the Volstead Act and state legislation merely required new imaginative methods of securing alcoholic beverages.

In the long run it was not only the widespread public acceptance of drinking that compromised and eventually killed

Prohibition, but also the failure to curb and control the availability of liquor from either smuggling or local manufacture. Even after 1925, when Congress allocated additional millions for liquor enforcement, rumrunning and illegal local manufacture of beer and whiskey continued on a massive scale. In one single month in May 1927 more than 400,000 cases of Canadian whiskey arrived in Detroit from Ontario.[1] During the period from April 1, 1927, to March 31, 1928, a total of 3,101,820 gallons of Canadian beer and whiskey and an additional 268,694 gallons of foreign beer, whiskey, and wine were exported from Windsor, Ontario. The estimated value of these liquor exports exceeded $20 million.[2] Even these figures, as large as they are, do not reflect the total quantity of Canadian liquor smuggled into Michigan. In addition to the volume transported from the Windsor export docks, hundreds of thousands of gallons were smuggled into Michigan hidden in railroad freight cars or in trucks that originated in other Canadian cities. The successful operation of rumrunners is revealed in a federal report in 1928 which indicated that only 5 percent of liquor smuggled into the United States was intercepted by enforcement agents. Evidence also indicates that the manufacture of alcoholic beverages in illegal stills matched the volume smuggled into Michigan.[3]

As the failure of the enforcement of the Eighteenth Amendment became widely recognized, many Americans looked for an explanation for the uncontrolled smuggling and the familiar operation of neighborhood speakeasies, blind pigs, and stills. Federal Prohibition agents and local police officers became the scapegoats and received much of the blame, especially from anti–saloon and temperance organizations. Although there were many dishonest, corrupt, and incompetent enforcement agencies, the great majority were dedicated and honest. During the Prohibition years in Michigan alone, enforcement agents made more than a hundred thousand arrests for violation of the Volstead Act and Michigan liquor laws. The dockets of local and U.S. District courts in southeastern Michigan were filled with liquor violations throughout the twenties.[4]

In retrospect, it is clear that although ineffective enforcement contributed to the failure to enforce Prohibition laws, even more important was the inability of the U.S. government to get the active support of Canada. By authorizing breweries and distilleries to operate at maximum capacity and because of lax export regulations, Canada presented U.S. enforcement agents with an impossible task. With several thousand miles of a poorly controlled border between Canada and the United States, Washington recognized this situation and constantly put pressure on Ottawa to change its policies relating to the manufacture and export of liquor. Even the Canadian levy of a nine dollar tax on each gallon of whiskey exported to a Prohibition country did little to stop smuggling. The Canadian government based its position upon several factors. Ottawa officials maintained that smuggling was a U.S. problem since the great majority of rumrunners were American. They were reluctant to close distilleries and breweries because of the tax revenue and the potential loss of tens of thousands of jobs. The manufacture of beer and whiskey was a major industry in Ottawa, just as rumrunning and the consumption of those beverages were second only to the automobile industry in Michigan.[5]

Finally in 1924, after lengthy negotiations, the United States and Canada signed a treaty designed to control some smuggling of liquor into the United States. Under the terms of the agreement Canadian officials would notify U.S. customs when a clearance was granted to a U.S. vessel to pick up liquor at Canadian export docks. The names of the vessels, their masters, and the quantity and type of cargo would be forwarded to U.S. Customs. This agreement fell far short of what the United States wanted—a complete embargo on all liquor shipments to the United States—but it was viewed as a step in the right direction, at least on paper. In practice, it did little to curb smuggling. The relevant information was forwarded to U.S. Customs officials, but it was often not received until after the liquor had been picked up, too late to assist in the capture of rumrunners. Furthermore, even when the data was for-

warded promptly, smugglers discovered other ways to avoid detection. Rumrunners changed the names on boats as soon as they cleared export docks, and they followed circuitous routes to avoid the Coast Guard and police patrol boats.

The customs records reveal the ineffectiveness of those new regulations. On a summer afternoon in 1928 Canadian authorities notified U.S. Customs of the clearance of five U.S. vessels from Detroit River export docks. Vessels named *Ben, Rat, Rabbit, Bird,* and *Bat* contained full cargoes of Canadian beer, wine, brandy, whiskey, and bourbon. Despite the warnings, none of the vessels were located, nor was any of the liquor ever found or confiscated.[6] It is possible that the rumrunners outran the Prohibition Navy on that day or perhaps enforcement officials were bribed. There is substantial data to support the latter explanation, especially from a Canadian Minister of Revenue who visited Windsor in the fall of 1928 to investigate firsthand reports of rumrunning on the Detroit River. With the aid of local Windsor contacts he was allowed aboard a "liquor export" vessel to observe rumrunning in action. He interrogated the vessel's crew about the finer points of smuggling. In answer to his question of whether they crossed the Detroit River during daytime hours, he received the reply, "Yes, quite often." "How is it they do not get you?" was his next query. The smuggler replied with a smile, "It just happens they are not there when we go across."[7]

Canada further complicated U.S. Prohibition enforcement plans in 1927 when the province of Ontario repealed its Prohibition regulations and authorized the legal sale and consumption in Ontario. This action had an immediate impact along the entire Michigan–Ontario waterway and indeed the rest of the border between the United States and Canada. Thousands of Michigan residents poured into Windsor, Sarnia, Sault Ste. Marie, and other Ontario cities and ports to purchase beer, wine, and whiskey. The demand for Canadian liquor increased so sharply that in June 1927 provincial liquor stores and outlets were forced to limit sales of whiskey to one case per person. The opening of the Ambassador Bridge in November 1929 and the Detroit–Windsor Tunnel a year later provided Detroiters even another avenue for smuggling choice Canadian beer and whiskey.[8]

Washington officials, including President Herbert Hoover, continued to pressure the Canadian government for further concessions and, in 1929, succeeded in persuading Ottawa to close down all export docks on the Detroit River and other border crossings. This action, along with stepped–up U.S. Coast Guard patrols, cut sharply into rumrunning along sections of the Detroit River, but did not eliminate smuggling or the availability of liquor. Smugglers simply changed their main routes to Lake St. Clair, the St. Clair River, and Lake Huron. They also used airplanes, trains, and trucks more exten-

sively. Furthermore, the slack was taken up by an increase in the local manufacture of beer and hard liquor.[9]

By 1930 public opinion in Michigan and in the northern industrial states was moving rapidly in favor of changes in the Volstead Act and even the repeal of the Eighteenth Amendment. The abject failure to stop smuggling and the illegal local manufacture of beer, wine, and hard liquor in commercial and home stills was the lesser catalyst for these changes. Even more influential was the public abhorrence of the crime and violence associated with Prohibition. Daily newspapers, magazines, radio, and other media gave special attention to the violent acts of criminals, the bribery and collusion of police and enforcement officials, and the violations of the Volstead Act.

In 1929 and 1930 Detroiters were exposed daily to a steady diet of gang violence, murder, and other liquor–related crimes. Detroit newspapers and local radio stations extensively covered the infamous St. Valentine's Day Massacre in February 1929 in Chicago. The murders resulted from the hijacking of a shipment of expensive Canadian whiskey smuggled across the Detroit River enroute to Al Capone's criminal empire in Cook County, Illinois. The summer of 1930 found Detroit the center of attention in gang warfare. In a month described by the press as "Bloody July," a number of rival gang members, all involved in liquor smuggling, were murdered followed by the execution type slaying of the popular radio commentator, Jerry Buckley, in a downtown Detroit hotel. The "Collingwood Massacre," as it was called in Detroit newspapers, involving rival rumrunners, further shocked Detroit residents.[10]

As the decade of the 1920s came to a close thousands of Michigan citizens, stunned and repelled by the rampant violence, joined organizations fighting for revisions of the Volstead Act. The boating and fishing interests represented by various clubs and associations also voiced their concerns about the enforcement practices of federal, state, and local policing agencies. Many Detroit pleasure boaters had become innocent victims of smugglers as well as trigger–happy enforcement officers. By 1929 the situation on the Detroit River and Lake St. Clair was so dangerous that the Detroit Yachting Association, representing many wealthy and influential Detroiters, sent a vigorous protest to Congress describing the "dangers of innocent persons being killed or wounded by indiscriminate shooting on the River and adjoining lakes." The bitterness of the allegations continued with the charge that the "swarming, sneaking agents have terrorized thousands of people who use our waters . . . for boating and fishing."[11]

The Automobile Club of Michigan—also representing an influential group of Michigan residents—added its concern to the litany of complaints about the practices of federal officials. They demanded that Congress investigate the "overzealous" actions of U.S. Customs agents for their "reckless searching of automobiles on the Detroit–Windsor ferries."[12]

Prominent Detroiters also complained about the actions of federal and state enforcement officials. As mentioned earlier, Henry B. Joy, former president of the Packard Motor Company and an influential business and community leader, became so incensed at the frequent federal raids on his boathouse on Lake St. Clair that he appealed directly to the Secretary of the Treasury and other friends in Washington. His first complaints went unheeded, but he kept up his attack on the Prohibition Unit of the Department of the Treasury. In 1928 Joy went even further and expressed his views publicly. In describing the situation along the Detroit River–St. Clair waterway, he charged that "crime is rampant and reverence for the Constitution is at its lowest ebb. It is the duty of every American who loves his country to strive for repeal of the Eighteenth Amendment and the restoration of the basic principles of American government, formerly guaranteed by the Constitution to every citizen."[13]

The strong public position espoused by Joy was especially significant, not only for its vitriolic tone but because Joy represented the views of a number of prominent Detroiters who had switched positions on Prohibition. In 1916, when the Prohibition amendment to the

Michigan Constitution was being considered, Joy was one of its outspoken supporters. James Couzens, former mayor of Detroit and U.S. senator from 1922 to 1930, also changed his views on Prohibition. By 1923 he had become so thoroughly disillusioned about the effectiveness of the Volstead Act that he endorsed legislation to legalize 5 percent beer and wine.[14] Although his public views brought charges by the Anti–Saloon League that he was a "traitor to America," he continued his opposition to Prohibition.[15] The prominent Frederick Alger family of Grosse Pointe, former Governor Fred Green, and Alfred Sloan, president of General Motors, also actively campaigned for the repeal of the Eighteenth Amendment.[16]

In addition to the complaints of boating and automobile associations and private citizens, organizations were established to fight specifically for the repeal of the Eighteenth Amendment. As early as 1920 a national lobbying organization, the Association Against the Prohibition Amendment (AAPA), was founded to campaign for repeal of Prohibition. Statewide chapters of the AAPA were also organized to fight for changes in state liquor laws. In Michigan the group's initial objective was the legalization of the manufacture of "genuine" beer (5 percent alcohol) and light wine.[17]

The Crusaders, founded in 1929, and the Women's Organization for National Prohibition Reform (WONPR) were national in scope but also had strong and active chapters in Detroit. The Crusaders, drawn primarily from the ranks of the Republican Party, used their influence and resources to elect wet Republicans to local, state, and national office. Mrs. Fred Alger of Grosse Pointe headed the WONPR in Michigan. In 1932 the Michigan Repeal Fund Committee was founded to support "repeal" candidates in the forthcoming November election.[18]

By 1928 repeal had become a national and state political issue. The Democratic Party, led by Governor Alfred Smith of New York, campaigned in the 1928 presidential election for changes in state and federal laws which would give to states, "after approval by a referendum popular vote of its people," the right to manufacture and sell alcoholic beverages for home consumption. Herbert Hoover, who called Prohibition "a great social and economic experiment, noble in nature and far reaching in purpose," won in a landslide, but not because of his Prohibition stance.[19] A 1930 national poll by the *Literary Digest* showed only about 30 percent favoring the continuation of the Eighteenth Amendment.[20]

The Prohibition issue split the two major political parties in Michigan as well as nationally. In the 1930 statewide election, Wilbur Brucker, the Republican candidate for governor, strongly endorsed the Eighteenth Amendment and urged more stringent federal and state liquor laws. His Democratic opponent, William A.

Comstock, on the other hand, called for the repeal of the Eighteenth Amendment. The Republican Party and the pro–Eighteenth Amendment position won in 1930, but their victory was short lived. The Democratic Party, with strong anti–Prohibition planks, swept the national and state elections in 1932. William A. Comstock defeated Brucker by a majority of nearly two hundred thousand votes; his majority in Wayne County alone carried the rest of the state by ninety votes. The referendum to repeal state liquor laws and create a state liquor control commission also won handily by a majority of 547,243 votes.[21] On the national scene Franklin Roosevelt, a long–time opponent of Prohibition, swept the national election with an overwhelming majority of electoral votes.

What had happened in two years to change the mind of Michigan voters? Without question the deepening economic depression played a major role in the Democratic victories in 1932. Unemployment had reached 46 percent in 1931 and was a major factor in the election, but the Prohibition issue also influenced the voters greatly. Michigan residents were tired of the failure of Prohibition and the criminal activity associated with it. Furthermore, the legalization of beer, wine, and hard liquor, it was widely believed, would result in thousands of new jobs in Michigan at breweries, distilleries, and in saloons, taverns, and restaurants. In addition, Michigan would receive millions in taxes levied upon the manufacturers of liquor—funds which were now going to Canadian coffers.

Curiously, arguments presented fifteen years earlier on behalf of Prohibition were now being heard in favor of repeal. It was now argued that the legalization of liquor would reduce crime, lawlessness, and gang violence. Police forces would be sharply reduced and jails emptied if liquor was legalized. Arguments were even heard that Prohibition was responsible for the rise of communism and other radical movements, especially among the army of the unemployed. The repeal of Prohibition would end this threat to a democratic society.

The U.S. Congress reacted to the November elections by taking prompt action on the Prohibition issue. In February 1933 the U.S. Senate and House of Representatives passed, by the necessary two–thirds majority, a Constitutional amendment repealing the Prohibition Amendment. The amendment was forwarded to the various states for their approval by a three quarters vote. On April 10, 1933, delegates to the Michigan convention voted ninety–nine to one to endorse the Twenty-first Amendment, the first state to take such action.[22]

Governor William Comstock also took additional action in Michigan to respond to the wishes of Michigan citizens relating to Prohibition. In January 1933 he appointed a special bipartisan committee to advise him on liquor legislation. Acting on its recommendations, the Governor on April 4, 1933, proposed legislation to define 3.2 percent beer and wine as non–intoxicating and make it available in all counties of the state, except those that voted for exemption. The state legislature endorsed the proposal along with the establishment of license fees on liquor manufacturers and dealers and a levy of $1.25 tax on each barrel of beer manufactured or sold in Michigan. "Beer Gardens" were authorized, where beer could be sold to patrons sitting at tables. Bars were outlawed. After minor debate, these proposals were approved by the state legislature to take effect at 6 p.m. on May 11, 1933.[23]

A special exception added to the act authorized the sale of beer on the evening of May 10, 1933, for the American Legion Convention being held in Detroit. Operating under Permit #1, the Legion was given a special waiver to sell and serve genuine 3.2 percent beer at its annual convention. The widely publicized gala affair covered on radio station WJR featured dancing, four glee clubs, and a special "Bung starting ceremony in which Julius Stroh removed the bung from a Gilded Keg of Stroh Bohemian Beer." One

thousand tables and ten thousand beer glasses rented for the occasion assisted legionnaires in their celebrations. Before the eight–hour festivities ended, three hundred half barrels and five hundred cases of Stroh's beer were consumed by the happy throng of legionnaires.[24] On the following day Julius Stroh happily toasted Governor William Comstock with the first "legal" glass of beer produced at the Stroh Brewery in Detroit.[25]

Later in the year in December the state legislature approved the manufacture of beer and wine containing 5 percent alcohol and at the same time authorized the establishment of state liquor stores. On December 30, 1933, the legislature approved the manufacture and sale of whiskey in state liquor stores.

The Twenty–first Amendment repealed the Prohibition Amendment on December 5, 1933, when Utah became the thirty–sixth and last state to ratify the amendment. After nearly fourteen years, Prohibition passed out of existence. Smuggling ended abruptly and most speakeasies and blind pigs soon closed, unable now to meet the competition of taverns and restaurants. The "noble experiment" passed into history.

END PROHIBITION

This Association Is Endorsed By the Pulpit and the Press

We deplore the present lawless condition throughout the country —the so-called "crime-wave." BUT THE RESPONSIBILITY SHOULD BE PUT SQUARELY WHERE IT BELONGS. **PROHIBITION** created the illicit liquor traffic—the greatest crime breeder of all time.

CONGRESS endeavors to function according to the will of a majority of our citizens. Let it know where YOU stand by joining this Association.

IT IS NOT TOO LATE TO REPEAL THE VOLSTEAD LAW.

This is not a "wet" society. It does not advocate the return of the old saloon conditions. It stands for fairness, moderation and respect for the Constitution of our fathers.

THE DUES ARE ONLY ONE DOLLAR PER YEAR. We are accountable TO YOU for every cent received and spent.

YOU DO NOT HAVE TO WORK—just enroll and be counted. But your active aid will be welcomed if you can give it.

EVERY CITIZEN OF THIS STATE IS WELCOME.

Brewers, distillers and those who have made their living from the liquor trade are ineligible to voting membership, so that the Association may be free from a fair accusation of financial interest in the subject of its work.

This emblem is worn by Liberty-loving A m e r i c a n men and women.
20,000 new members every day right now.

It is not worn by the prohibition fanatic, the bootlegger, the moonshiner, or the spy.
Show your colors.

HOW YOUR $1.00 A YEAR MEMBERSHIP FEE IS SPENT

OFFICE HELP PRINT-RENT ETC.
NATIONAL ORGANIZATION AT WASHINGTON 25¢ 15¢ ENROLLING MEMBERSHIPS 10¢

MICHIGAN STATEWIDE MEMBERSHIP CAMPAIGN 50¢

JOIN TODAY!

Tear Off and Mail Right Now

(1) I accompany herewith One Dollar ($1.00), being my membership fee for one year from date in the Michigan Division of the National Association Against the Prohibition Amendment, and request that my name be placed upon the rolls of the Association.

(2) I am in favor of the repeal of the Volstead Act.

(3) I am opposed to the old type saloon and the indiscriminate retailing of intoxicating liquors.

(4) It is my firm intention, under normal conditions, to favor those legislative and congressional candidates who openly stand for the repeal of the Volstead Law and who favor states rights as to prohibition.

(5) (I reserve the right to resign at any time and to suspend this pledge, upon filing a letter to that effect with this Association for any given election when in my opinion the public interest justifies this course.)

ROBT. D. WARDELL, Sec.
MICHIGAN DIVISION

NATIONAL ASSOCIATION AGAINST THE PROHIBITION AMENDMENT

Return to Michigan Office, 231 Bagley Ave., Detroit, Mich.

(Please Write Plainly or Print)

....
Member

....
Address

State number of members you can secure. Blanks will be mailed to you.

If you desire that your membership shall not be made public, mark X in the following space........

Within months of the beginning of Prohibition, organized efforts were made for its repeal. Brewers and distillers were ineligible for membership in this association, December 3, 1921. Courtesy: *Detroit Saturday Night.*

Flood Time in Detroit

Newspaper cartoonists reflected public opinion towards the failure of enforcing Prohibition, *Detroit Saturday Night,* August 7, 1926.

As a result of strong pressure from Washington, the Canadian government closed liquor export docks in Ontario in 1929. Empty export docks, like this one in Windsor, marked a decline in smuggling on the Detroit River. Courtesy: *Windsor Star.*

After the repeal of Prohibition in Ontario in 1927, Michigan residents flocked to Windsor, Sarnia, Sault Ste. Marie, and other Ontario cities to purchase liquor and smuggle it into the United States. Courtesy: *Windsor Star.*

Young Windsor boys lined up with wagons outside of provincial liquor stores to assist customers in transporting whiskey and beer to their homes. Courtesy: *Detroit News.*

The end of Prohibition in Ontario in June 1927 brought hundreds of Windsorites to provincial liquor stores. This resident is waiting patiently in line for her supply of whiskey. The demand was so great that the government limited purchases. Courtesy: *Windsor Star.*

The excursion vessel *Ste. Claire* was caught in a cross fire with the border patrol in 1931. An innocent passenger was wounded on the deck of the *Ste. Claire* by stray bullets from a border patrol boat. Incidents like this helped sway public opinion against Prohibition. Courtesy: Dossin Great Lakes Museum.

Another victim of rumrunning was the steamer *Erie,* which burned with three vessels in Ecorse in February 1929. A "Rum Cigaret" was blamed for the fire. Courtesy: Dossin Great Lakes Museum.

This cartoon which appeared in *Outlook* and *Independent Magazine* called attention to the close public association between Prohibition and racketeers. Courtesy: *Detroit News.*

The Crusaders, founded in 1929, drawn primarily from the ranks of Republicans, helped elect wet candidates to local, state, and national offices. Courtesy: Library of Congress.

"Five Votes for Repeal." Five prominent Detroiters took an active role in the repeal campaign. Left to right: Mrs. C. A. Dean, Jr., Mrs. David McMorran, Mrs. Fred Alger, Mrs. Thomas F. McAllister, and Mrs. Catherine D. Doren. Courtesy: Burton Historical Collection.

The Detroit chapter of the Women's Organization for National Prohibition Reform, led by Mrs. Fred Alger of Grosse Pointe, was a powerful advocate of repeal. This poster gave women an opportunity to announce their views on Prohibition. Courtesy: *Detroit News.*

"Detroit Victory Day," May 10, 1933. Julius Stroh pouring the first legal glass of beer after Prohibition ended. In an eight–hour period during the American Legion Convention in Detroit, three hundred half barrels and five hundred cases of Stroh's beer were consumed by happy legion-naires. Courtesy: Associated Press.

Michigan Governor William Comstock purchased the first bottle of liquor (Old Taylor) on December 30, 1933. Detroit acting Mayor John Smith looks on. Courtesy: Burton Historical Collection.

First liquor sold at the Fort Shelby Hotel cocktail room, December 30, 1933. Courtesy: Burton Historical Collection.

Announcement

After an absence of over fifteen years, S T R O H ' S BOHEMIAN BEER will again be available to the people of Detroit and Michigan after 6:00 P. M. Thursday, May 11th.

During this long period we have kept our plant, as well as our organization, intact, because we felt that sooner or later the people of the United States and Michigan would recognize the evils of prohibition and would eventually again permit the sale of beer. We are very happy to see our hopes realized.

The STROH'S BOHEMIAN BEER which will be on sale this evening is equal, if not superior, to anything we have ever turned out in the pre-prohibition days, and we hope it will be enjoyed by everyone.

We wish to assure our many friends and the public at large that STROH'S BOHEMIAN BEER is manufactured up to a standard, and not down to a price, and that the quality will be maintained. We will not put out a single bottle or barrel of beer which has not been properly aged. This may cause inconvenience temporarily, but this has always been, and will continue to be, our policy. Strict adherence to these principles has earned for STROH'S BOHEMIAN BEER the title, "AMERICA'S FAVORITE."

The Stroh Products Co.

Julius Stroh, President

Stroh's Bohemian Beer was available within hours after the end of Prohibition. Courtesty: *Detroit Saturday Night,* May 10, 1933.

The end of Prohibition was the subject of numerous cartoons and newspaper stories. The *Toledo Morning Times* featured this illustration on July 4, 1933.

The *Detroit Saturday Night* cartoon of April 8, 1933, reflected the popular election in favor of repeal.

This Canadian Club advertisement with its snob appeal was featured in the *Detroit Saturday Night*, March 24, 1934.

NOTES

Chapter 1

1. For an account of the Prohibition movement in Michigan see George B. Catlin, *The Story of Detroit* (Detroit: *The Detroit News*, 1923), pp. 677–80. Roger Bruns provides an excellent survey of the Prohibition movement in the United States in *Preacher: Billy Sunday and Big Time Evangelism* (New York: W. W. Norton & Co., 1992). See also N. H. Bowen, "Liquor Fights Have Stirred Michigan for Over 75 Years," *Detroit Saturday Night*, December 10, 1921.

2. The most comprehensive study of Prohibition in Michigan is found in Larry Engelmann, *Intemperance, The Lost War Against Liquor* (New York: The Free Press, 1979).

3. Ibid., p. 14. According to Engelmann, the REO Motor Car Company secretly investigated the private lives of their workers and reported on those who smoked, drank, and voted against Prohibition. Allan Nevins, *Ford: The Times, The Man, The Company* (New York: Chas. Scribner's Sons, 1954), pp. 551–67.

4. Engelmann, "Billy Sunday: 'God, You've Got a Job on Your Hands in Detroit,'" *Michigan History*, LV (Spring 1971), pp. 1–23; Roger A. Bruns, *Preacher*, pp. 177–82.

5. Bruns, *Preacher*, p. 163.

6. Ibid., p. 154.

7. Quoted in Bruns, *Preacher*, p. 166.

8. Ibid., p. 179.

9. Ibid.

10. Ibid., p. 7.

11. McLoughlin, *Billy Sunday*, p. 147.

12. Charles Merz, *The Dry Decade* (New York: Doubleday, Doran & Co., 1932).

13. For a brief summary of the legislation acts relating to prohibition in Michigan, see Engelmann, "Booze: The Ohio Connection, 1918–1919," *Detroit in Perspective*, 2 (Winter 1975), p. 128.

14. Florence Odell Livingston Ledyard Collection, Burton Historical Collection, Detroit Public Library.

15. For a comprehensive account of the Ohio–Michigan liquor smuggling operation, see Engelmann, *Intemperance*, pp. 111–29.

16. Frank B. Elser, "Keeping Detroit on the Water Wagon," *The Outlook,* 121 (April 2, 1919), pp. 560–.

17. Ibid., p. 561.

18. For an account of the Billingsleys, see Engelmann, "Booze: The Ohio Connection," pp. 118–; "U.S. Law on Bootleggers," *Detroit News,* September 30, 1918, pp.1, 3; January 24, 1919.

19. *Detroit News,* January 24, 1919.

20. Elser, p. 562.

21. Ibid., p. 560.

22. Ibid. The Damon Law also provided for the closing of speakeasies or other illegal drinking establishments.

23. Ibid., p. 562.

24. Ibid.

25. Ibid.

26. "Michigan's 'Great Booze Rush' and its Suppression by State and Federal Action," *Literary Digest,* March 15, 1919, p. 85.

27. Ibid., pp. 85–86; Engelmann, "Booze: The Ohio Connection", pp. 124–26.

28. "Michigan's 'Great Booze Rush,'" pp. 85–90.

Chapter 2

1. For accounts of the campaign for the Eighteenth Amendment and its final passage, see Charles Merz, *The Dry Decade* (New York: Doubleday, Doran & Co., 1930); Engelmann, *Intemperance;* and Frederick Lewis Allen, *Only Yesterday* (New York: Harper & Bros., 1931); Joseph R. Gusfield, *Symbolic Crusade Status Politics and the American Temperance Movement* (Urbana, IL: University of Illinois Press, 1963).

2. McLoughlin, *Billy Sunday,* 147; Robert Conot, *American Odyssey* (New York: Wm. Morrow & Co., 1974), p. 215.

3. *New York Times,* January 17, 1920.

4. Allen, *Only Yesterday,* p. 248.

5. For accounts of Prohibition in Canada, and especially the Windsor–Amherstberg area of Ontario, see C. H. Gervais, *The Rumrunners: A Prohibition Scrapbook* (Scarborough, Ontario: Firefly Books, 1980); Engelmann, *Intemperance,* pp. 70–78.

6. Gervais, *Rumrunners Scrapbook,* p. 9. In April 1921 Ontario passed legislation prohibiting the importation of liquor from outside of the province. This act did not end the consumption of liquor in Windsor, Amhersburg, and other Ontario communities. It only encouraged illegal rumrunning from Michigan and Quebec. Gerald Hallowell, "Prohibition in Ontario" (M.A. Thesis: Carleton University, 1966).

7. Engelmann, *Intemperance,* pp. 77–78.

8. Robert Carse, *Rum Row* (New York: Rinehart & Co., 1959); Malcolm Willoughby, *Rum War at Sea* (Washington, D.C.: U.S. Government Printing Office, 1964); Irving King, "U.S. Coast Guard in the Rum War," Typescript, 1993, Dossin Great Lakes Museum; Harvey Patton, "Gun Fights Frequent in Whiskey Running on Mexican Border," *Detroit Saturday Night,* May 7, 1921.

9. The estimates of the volume of Canadian liquor smuggled into the United States varied. There is no question that by 1925 the great percentage of illegal liquor was smuggled into the Detroit area. The June 11, 1929, *New York Times* reported that 85 percent of the liquor coming from Canada into the United States came through the Detroit area.

10. "'Shooting' Detroit Bootleggers—with a Camera," *Literary Digest,* December 29, 1923, p. 35.

11.Ibid.

12. Engelmann, *Intemperance,* p. 72.

13. Gervais, *Rumrunners Scrapbook,* p. 10.; Engelmann, *Intemperance,* p. 73.

14. In an excellent comprehensive series of feature articles on rumrunning in May 1928, the *Detroit News* described in some detail the various signalling techniques used by smugglers on the Detroit River and Lake St. Clair. "Flashing Signals Guide Smugglers Across River," *Detroit News,* May 2, 1928.

15. *New York Times,* June 23, 1929; Engelmann, *Intemperance,* pp. 151–52.

16. Engelmann, *Intemperance,* pp. 113–18. The *New York Times* reported on December 1, 1928, that smugglers paid police five hundred dollars for a "free night" when they could work in safety; King, E–18; Jill Carson, "When Booze was Illegal," *Port Huron Times Herald,* February 4, 1990.

17. Engelmann, *Intemperance,* p. 90.

18. *New York Times,* January 18, 1925.

19. Engelmann, *Intemperance,* pp. 78–79.

20. Ibid., p. 88; *New York Times,* March 9, 1933.

21. *New York Times,* September 15, 1929.

22. *New York Times,* May 18, 1920.

23. Gervais, *Rumrunners Scrapbook,* pp. 17–18; Engelmann, *Intemperance,* pp. 87–88.

24. *New York Times,* November 19, 1930; Engelmann, *Intemperance,* pp. 84–85.

25. Gervais, *Rumrunners Scrapbook,* pp. 17–18; Engelmann, *Intemperance,* pp. 86–87; *New York Times,* June 21, 1923, June 4, 1927.

26. *New York Times,* May 27, 1928.

27. *New York Times,* June 25, 1922, May 27, 1928.

28. Elser, "Keeping Detroit on the Water Wagon," p. 560.

29. *New York Times,* June 25, 1922.

30. *New York Times,* May 17, 1920.

31. *New York Times,* June 25, 1927.

Chapter 3

1. Woodford, *All Our Yesterdays,* p. 303.

2. For one of the finest accounts of the 1920s, see Frederick Lewis Allen's *Only Yesterday.*

3. F. Clever Bald, *Michigan In Four Centuries* (New York: Harper & Row, 1954), pp. 394–99; Arthur Woodford, *Detroit American Urban Renaissance* (Tulsa, Ok: Continental Heritage, Inc., 1979), p. 106; Olivier Zunz, *The Changing Face of Inequality* (Chicago: University of Chicago Press, 1982), p. 287.

4. Woodford, *Detroit: American Urban Renaissance,* p. 111; W. Hawkins Ferry, *Buildings of Detroit* (Detroit: Wayne State University Press, 1958), p. 328.

5. For a chronology of key events relating to Detroit during prohibition, see Rae E. Rips, ed., *Detroit in Its World Setting* (Detroit: Detroit Public Library, 1953), pp. 223–67.

6. Ibid.; Allen, *Only Yesterday,* pp. 76–84.

7. Allen, *Only Yesterday,* pp. 88–122.

8. Ibid., p. 99.

9. Ibid., pp. 110–11.

10. Engelmann, *Intemperance,* pp. 125–37.

11. Woodford, *All our Yesterdays,* pp. 305–6; Mary Karshner, "Blossom Heath," *Muskrat Tales* V (Spring 1988), pp. 10–18; Malcolm Bingay, *Detroit is My Own Home Town* (New York: Bobbs Merrill, 1946), p. 323; Conot; *American Odyssey,* p. 215. Representatives of the Michigan Law Enforcement League visited speakeasies in all sections of the greater Detroit area and reported their location, hours, and activities to the Federal Prohibition Service. Scores of raids resulted from this data. Michigan Law Enforcement League, "Bulletin" in Governor Fred Green Papers, Michigan State Archives.

12. "When Booze Was Illegal," Port Huron *Times Herald,* February 5, 1990.

13. Jill Carson, "Speak Easy Keeps Wolf from the Family Door."

14. "When Booze Was Illegal."

15. Karshner, "Blossom Heath," pp. 1–18; Woodford, *All Our Yesterdays,* p. 305.

16. Engelmann, *Intemperance,* p. 131.

17. Woodford, p. 306; R. J. McLoughlin, "Ecorse, Thanks to Mr. Volstead, Finds the River a Stream of Gold," *Detroit Saturday Night,* August 20, 1921, pp. 3–4.

18. Karshner, "Blossom Heath," p. 10–18; Michigan State Police, "Captain Leonard's Squads," Michigan State Archives; Grosse Pointe Park Police Records, 1927–1930.

19. Frank Woodford, *Alex J. Groesbeck* (Detroit: Wayne State University Press, 1962), pp. 177–78; Engelmann, *Intemperance,* pp. 157–58; Arthur E.

Wood, *Hamtramck: A Sociological Study of a Polish-American Community* (New Haven, CT: College & University Press, 1955), p. 49; Alex Groesbeck Papers, Michigan State Archives, August 5, 1924.

20. Bingay, *Detroit Is My Own Home Town,* p. 323.

21. Coleman Young, *Hard Stuff: Autobiography of Coleman Young* (New York: Viking Press, 1994), p. 21.

22. Governor Fred Green Papers, Prohibition Files 1927–1929, Michigan State Archives.

23. Ibid.

24. Engelmann, *Intemperance,* pp. 134–35.

25. *New York Times,* May 27, 1928.

26. Bingay, *Detroit Is My Own Home Town,* p. 323.

27. "Prohibition Reported Winning in the Colleges," *Literary Digest,* June 7, 1924; Engelmann, *Intemperance,* pp. 171–73.

28. Woodford, *All Our Yesterdays,* p. 304; *New York Times,* June 25, 1922.

29. *Detroit News,* June 8, 1918; Merz, *Dry Decade,* pp. 65–66.

30. Merz, *Dry Decade,* pp. 66–67; Allen, *Only Yesterday,* p. 249; Engelmann, *Intemperance,* p. 137.

31. Engelmann, *Intemperance,* p. 139.

32. Ibid., p. 138.

33. Ibid.

34. Merz, *Dry Decade,* pp. 69–71.

35. Ibid., pp. 68–69.

36. Woodford, *All Our Yesterdays,* p. 304.

37. Engelmann, *Intemperance,* pp. 178–81; Engelmann, "The Iron River Rum Rebellion," *Mid-America* 55 (January 1973), pp. 37–53.

Chapter 4

1. Irving King, "The U.S. Coast Guard in the Rum War," Typescript, Dossin Great Lakes Museum, E–1.

2. Gervais, *Rumrunners Scrapbook,* pp. 11–13.

3. King, "U.S. Coast Guard," E–1.

4. Engelmann, *Intemperance,* p. 78.

5. Ibid. Among other rumrunners captured by enforcement officials and recommissioned for patrol against smugglers were the *Aladdin* and *Vedas.*

6. Ibid., p. 81.

7. Cynthia Bieniek, "Rumrunning Days on Lake St. Clair," *Muskrat Tales* 6 (Winter 1993), p. 17; Engelmann, *Intemperance,* pp. 112–13; *Detroit Free Press,* April 14, 1929.

8. Engelmann, *Intemperance,* pp. 99–100. Another famous incident involved the fatal accidental shooting of William Niedermeier, a sixty-five-year-old rural letter carrier, who was shot in the back on December 3, 1926, as "he sat in his dock skiff and died in terrible agony in a few days." *Congressional Record,* Vol. 71 (Pt. 3), June 17, 1929, p. 2992; Edgar G. Gordon to W. W. Potter, January 8, 1927, State Attorney General Files, Michigan State Archives.

9. Engelmann, *Intemperance,* p. 102. For additional information on Joy's complaints against federal liquor enforcement officials, see Joy correspondence in Governor Fred Green Papers, February 1928, Michigan State Archives.

10. Engelmann, *Intemperance,* p. 118.

11. King, "U.S. Coast Guard," E–18.

12. *New York Times,* December 1, 1928; *Detroit Free Press,* November 29 and 30, December 2 and 14, 1928; *Detroit News,* November 30, December 1 and 2, 1928; *Detroit Times,* December 2, 1928.

13. Engelmann, *Intemperance,* p. 118.

14. Ibid., p. 108.

15. Jill Carson, "When Booze was Illegal," *Port Huron Times Herald,* February 4, 1990.

16. Ibid.

17. Ibid.

18. Ibid.

19. *Congressional Record,* Vol. 69 (Pt. 2), January 16, 1928, p. 1528.

20. Woodford, *All Our Yesterdays,* pp. 306–10; Engelmann, *Intemperance,* pp. 142–47; Allen, *Only Yesterday,* pp. 259–69; Gervais, *Rumrunners Scrapbook,* pp. 31–146; Robert Schoenberg, *Mr. Capone* (New York: Wm. Morrow & Co., 1994); John Kobler, *Capone* (New York: G. P. Putnam's Sons, 1971).

21. R. J. McLauchlin, "Ecorse, Thanks to Mr. Volstead Finds the River a Stream of Gold," *Detroit Saturday Night,* August 20, 1921; Engelmann, *Intemperance,* pp. 105–11; Woodford, *All Our Yesterdays,* pp. 305–6; F. L. Smith, "War on the River," *Outlook,* July 24, 1929.

22. McLauchlin, "Ecorse."

23. "`Shooting' Detroit Bootleggers—With a Camera," *Literary Digest,* December 23, 1923, p. 36. Engelman, *Intemperance,* pp. 109–10; *New York Times,* July 15, 1923.

24. Woodford, *Alex Groesbeck,* p. 177.

25. Ibid.

26. Woodford, *All Our Yesterdays,* p. 177; Wood, *Hamtramck,* p. 49; Engelmann, *Intemperance,* pp. 157–58; R. A. Haynes to Governor Alex Groesbeck, August 25, 1924, Groesbeck Papers, Michigan State Archives.

27. Woodford, *All Our Yesterdays,* p. 177; Engelmann, *Intemperance,* pp. 157–58; *New York Times,* June 8, 1926.

28. "City's Record on Prohibition," *Detroit News,* May 14, 1928.

Chapter 5

1. *New York Times,* June 4, 1927.

2. *Detroit News,* May 6, 1928.

3. *New York Times,* June 11, 1929. According to Canadian officials, only 10 percent of illegal liquor consumed in the United States was smuggled from Canada. They estimated that the overwhelming amount—90 percent—was produced in the United States. *Congressional Record,* Vol. 71, (Pt. 2), June 3, 1929, p. 2254.

4. For an idea of the number and types of violations of the Volstead Act, see the Arthur J. Tuttle Collection, Bentley Library, University of Michigan. Tuttle was U.S. District Judge for the Eastern District of Michigan from 1912 to 1944. He presided over thousands of such cases.

5. Gervais, *Rumrunners Scrapbook,* pp. 9–19.

6. *Congressional Record,* V. 71 (Pt. 2), June 3, 1929, p. 2251.

7. Ibid., p. 2256.

8. *New York Times,* June 4, 1927.

9. *New York Times,* July 8, 1929; November 19, 1930.

10. Woodford , pp. 306–10; Gervais, *Rumrunners Scrapbook,* pp. 133–46; Allen, *Only Yesterday,* pp. 259–69.

11. *Congressional Record,* Vol. 71 (Pt. 3), June 17, 1929, p. 2992.

12. Ibid.

13. Henry B. Joy to Hon. Louis Cuvellier, February 2, 1928, in Governor Fred Green Papers, Michigan State Archives.

14. Harry Barnard, *Independent Man: The Life of Senator James Couzens* (New York: Scribner's, 1958), pp. 152–53.

15. Ibid.

16. Engelmann, *Intemperance,* p. 204.

17. Ibid., pp. 189–220.

18. Ibid. pp. 207–8.

19. Allen, *Only Yesterday,* p. 256.

20. Lewis Frederick Allen, *Since Yesterday* (New York: Harper & Row, 1939), p. 33.

21. Engelmann, *Intemperance,* pp. 218–33.

22. Allen, *Since Yesterday,* pp. 99–100.

23. Engelmann, *Intemperance,* pp. 220–21.

24. *Detroit News,* May 10, 1937.

25. Engelmann, *Intemperance,* p. 221.

GLOSSARY OF PROHIBITION TERMS

Ante–Volstead:

Before the days of Prohibition; liquor that was produced before the Volstead Law went into effect; real liquor.

Apple–jack:

Brandy made from apples; any intoxicating liquor.

Baptized:

Diluted liquor.

Barrel house:

A place where liquor is sold illegally.

Barrel–house bum:

A drunkard.

Beerage:

Prominent people whose wealth has come from the manufacture and sale of beer.

Beerocracy:

People who have made fortunes by the manufacture and sale of beer. A member of this group is a beerocrat.

Beery:

Slightly intoxicated.

Bingo:

Intoxicating liquor.

Bleary–eyed:

Intoxicated.

Blind pig or Blind tiger:

A place where liquor is sold illegally. Term originated from the practice of a shrewd Yankee who evaded law against the sale of liquor by placing a blind pig on a box inside of a tented enclosure and announced, "See the blind pig. Ten cents a look." With each payment he gave away a drink of rye or bourbon.

Blue pig:

Whiskey.

Blue ruin:

Poor gin.

Boilermaker's delight:

Poor whiskey; moonshine.

Bootleg:

To sell liquor illegally; liquor that is sold illegally.

Bootlegger:

One who sold liquor illegally. Term originally applied to one who hid liquor in his boot legs.

Booze:

Intoxicating liquor; to drink it.

Booze fest:

A drinking party.

Boozery:

A place where liquor is sold, especially a place where it is sold illegally.

Cider drunk:

A drinker of hard cider; intoxication produced by hard cider.

Corked:

Intoxicated.

Demon rum:

Intoxicating liquor.

Dive:

A place where liquor is sold illegally.

Doggery:

A place where liquor is sold illegally.

Drug story whiskey:

Whiskey bought with a prescription.

Dry:

A person who is opposed to allowing the sale of intoxicating liquors.

Embalmed:

Highly intoxicated.

Eye opener:

A drink of liquor, especially one taken shortly after getting up in the morning.

Flapper:

Young female of the 1920s. Term signified young woman with a cynical attitude; an interest in daring fashions and indifferent morals.

Gin mill:

A low dive; a saloon.

Heeby–jeebies:

Delirium tremens.

High jinks:

A drunken carousal.

Hooch:

Intoxicating liquor.

Jackass brandy:

Homemade brandy with a powerful kick.

Jimmy:

A blind pig; an illegal saloon.

Joint:
A place where liquor was sold illegally.

Juniper juice:
Intoxicating liquor.

yKid:
A flask of liquor.

Liquorsham Commission:
The Wickersham Commission.

Loaded for bear:
Highly intoxicated.

Long pull:
A large drink, especially from a flask.

Monkey swill:
Intoxicating liquor.

Moon:
Whiskey; intoxicating liquor.

Moonshine:
Intoxicating liquor.

Moonshiner's gopher:
A man who peddles illegal liquor.

Mule:
Corn alcohol; whiskey; intoxicating liquor.

Panther sweat:
Intoxicating liquor.

Pocket pistol:
A liquor flask.

Pop highball:
Soda water with alcohol added.

Pull a Daniel Boone:
To get intoxicated.

Red eye:
Intoxicating liquor.

Rumhole:
A saloon.

Rye sap:
Intoxicating liquor; whiskey.

Schooner:
A place where liquor is sold illegally.

Shoe polish:
Whiskey.

Shoe polish shop:
An illicit saloon.

Speakeasy:
A place where liquor was sold illegally or after legal hours. Term first used in the nineteenth century to mean "speak softly when ordering illicit liquor."

Squirrel:
Whiskey.

Squirrel dew:
Intoxicating liquor.

Three fingers in a bathtub:
A large drink of whiskey.

Three sheets in the wind:

Intoxicated.

Wet:

A person who is in favor of allowing the sale of intoxicating liquors.

Whale:

A heavy drinker.

White coffee:

Whiskey; strong drink; liquor that is sold illegally.

White lightning:

Intoxicating liquor.

Wickedsham Commission:

The Wickersham Commission.

The information on Prohibition terms was taken from newspaper articles and literature of the 1920s and the following sources: Chapman, Robert L., *New Dictionary of American Slang* (New York: Harper and Row, 1986); Horwill, H. W., *A Dictionary of American Usage* (London: Oxford Press, 1935); Wentworth, Harold, and Stuart B. Flexner, *Dictionary of American Slang* (New York: Thomas Crowell Co., 1968); Weseen, Maurice H., *A Dictionary of American Slang* (New York: Thomas Y. Crowell, 1935).

SELECTED BIBLIOGRAPHY

Published Sources

U.S. General

Because of the significance and popular appeal of the subject matter, a vast amount of published material is available on the temperance and Prohibition movements in the United States and Canada. Hundreds of writers, including academic scholars, journalists, clergy, and novelists have devoted their attention to these subjects. The first comprehensive published studies to appear were Charles Merz, *The Dry Decade* (New York: Doubleday, Doran & Co., 1932), and John A. Krout, *Origins of Prohibition* (New York: A.A. Knopf, 1925). They are still valuable sources. More recent general studies include: Joseph R. Gusfield, *Symbolic Crusade: Status Politics and the American Temperance Movement* (Urbana, IL: University of Illinois Press, 1963); Norman Clark, *Deliver Us From Evil: An Interpretation of American Prohibition* (New York: W. W. Norton & Co., 1976); Andrew Sinclair, *Era of Excess: A Social History of the Prohibition Movement* (New York: Harper & Row, 1964); James Timberlake, *Prohibition and the Progressive Movement, 1900–1920* (Cambridge: Harvard University Press, 1963); Herbert Asbury, *The Great Illusion: An Informal History of Prohibition* (New York: Doubleday, 1950); Thomas M. Coffey, *The Long Thirst: Prohibition in America* (New York: Norton, 1975); John Kobler, *Ardent Spirits: The Rise and Fall of Prohibition* (New York: Putnam, 1973); and Kenneth Allsop, *The Bootleggers and Their Era* (Garden City, NY: Arlington House, 1961).

The role of the U.S. Coast Guard in enforcing Prohibition is found in numerous studies including: Malcolm Willoughby, *Rum War at Sea* (Washington, D.C.: Government Printing Office, 1964); Robert Carse, *Rum Row* (New York: Rinehart & Co., 1959); Karl Baarslag, *Coast Guard to the Rescue* (Chicago: Cadmus Books, 1936); Irving King, "U.S. Coast Guard in the Rum War," typescript (1993) in Dossin Great Lakes Museum Library; and Harold Waters, *Smugglers and Spirits:*

173

Prohibition and the Coast Guard Patrol (New York: Hastings House, 1971).

Several books devoted to the first four decades of the twentieth century give special attention to Prohibition, including: Frederick Lewis Allen, *Only Yesterday: An Informal History of the Nineteen Twenties* (New York: Harper & Bros., 1931) and *Since Yesterday: The Nineteen Thirties in America* (New York: Harper & Row, 1940); and Francis Russell, *The Shadow of Blooming Grove: Warren G. Harding in His Times* (New York: McGraw–Hill, 1968).

The role of the charismatic evangelist Billy Sunday in the campaign for Prohibition is found in William G. McLoughlin, Jr., *Billy Sunday Was His Real Name* (Chicago: University of Chicago Press, 1955) and in a magnificent study by Roger Bruns, *Preacher Billy Sunday and Big Time Evangelism* (New York: W. W. Norton & Co., 1992).

The gangster Al Capone is given attention in John Kobler, *Capone* (New York: G. P. Putnam Sons, 1971); Robert Schoenberg, *Mr. Capone* (New York: Wm. Morrow & Co., 1994); and especially in the delightful account by Leonard N. Simons, " Prohibition and the Purple Gang," unpublished manuscript, February 1994. See also Neal Shine, "Distilled Memories: The Purple Gang's Business Was Booze," *Detroit Free Press,* March 27, 1994.

The hundreds of slang expressions that relate to Prohibition are found in: Robert L. Chapman, *New Dictionary of American Slang* (New York: Harper and Row, 1986); H. W. Horwill, *A Dictionary of American Usage* (London: Oxford University Press, 1935); Harold Wentworth and Stuart B. Flexner, *Dictionary of American Slang* (New York: Thomas Crowell Co., 1968); and Maurice H. Weseen, *A Dictionary of American Slang* (New York: Thomas Y. Crowell, 1935).

Michigan

The finest and most exhaustive work on Prohibition in Michigan has been done by Larry Engelmann. His Ph.D. dissertation, "O Whiskey: The History of Prohibition in Michigan" (University of Michigan, 1971) was followed by the comprehensive study *Intemperance: The Lost War Against Liquor* (New York: The Free Press, 1979). Engelmann dealt with other aspects of Prohibition in other publications, including: " Billy Sunday: God You've Got a Job on Your Hands," *Michigan History* LV (Spring 1971) 1–23; "A Separate Peace: The Politics of Prohibition Enforcement in Detroit, 1928–1930," *Detroit in Perspective* I (Autumn 1972) 51–73; "Booze: The Ohio Connection, 1918–1919," *Detroit in Perspective: A Journal of Regional History* II (Winter 1975) 111–28; and "The Iron River Rum Rebellion," *Mid America* 55 (January 1973) 37–53.

For a more recent account of rumrunning on the Detroit River, see Philip P. Mason, "Anyone Who Couldn't Get a Drink Wasn't Trying: Rumrunning Along the Michigan–Ontario Border During Prohibition," *Michigan History* 78 (Sep–Oct 1994) 12–22; and Paul Labadie, "Liquid Gold," *Michigan History* 78 (Sep–Oct 1994) 25–26.

General studies of Detroit and its institutions have also given special attention to the 1920s and Prohibition in Michigan. See, for example: F. Clever Bald, *Michigan in Four Centuries* (New York: Harper and Bros., 1954); Frank and Arthur Woodford, *All Our Yesterdays* (Detroit: Wayne State University Press, 1969); Arthur Woodford, *Detroit: American Urban Renaissance* (Tulsa, OK: Continental Heritage, Inc., 1979); Robert Conot, *American Odyssey* (New York: Wm. Morrow & Co., 1974); Rae Ripps, ed., *Detroit In Its World Setting* (Detroit: Detroit Public Library, 1953); Harry Barnard, *Independent Man: The Life of Senator James Couzens* (New York: Scribner's, 1958); Frank Woodford, *Alex J. Groesbeck, Portrait of a Public Man* (Detroit: Wayne State University Press, 1962); John C. Lodge, *I Remember Detroit* (Detroit: Wayne State University Press, 1949); Keith Sward, *The Legend of Henry Ford* (New York: Rinehart, 1948); Allan Nevins, *Ford: The Times, the Man, the Company* (New York: Chas. Scribner's Sons, 1954); Malcolm Bingay, *Detroit Is My Own Home Town* (New York: Bobbs, Merrill, 1946); George Catlin, *The Story of Detroit* (Detroit: *The Detroit News*, 1923); Olivier Zunz, *The Changing Face of Inequality* (Chicago: University of Chicago Press, 1982); W. Hawkins Ferry, *Buildings of Detroit* (Detroit: Wayne State University Press, 1968); Arthur E. Wood, *Hamtramck: A Sociological Study of a Polish–American Community* (New Haven, CT: College & University Press, 1955); Oscar Olander, *Michigan State Police: A Twenty–Five Year History* (East Lansing: Michigan Police Journal Press, 1942); and Coleman Young, *Hard Stuff: Autobiography of Coleman Young* (New York: Viking Press, 1994).

From the beginning of Prohibition, smuggling on the Michigan–Ontario waterway, and on especially the Detroit River, attracted the attention of national newspapers and journals. Feature writers and journalists were sent to Detroit during Prohibition to cover the Detroit smuggling scene. Of special interest are: "Michigan's 'Great Booze Rush' and its Suppression by State and Federal Action," *The Literary Digest* (March 15, 1919) 80–90; Frank B. Esler, "Keeping Detroit on the Water Wagon," *The Outlook* 121 (April 2, 1919) 560–67; Winthrop D. Lane, "Prohibition: What Elimination of the Liquor Traffic Means to Grand Rapids?" *Survey* XLV (Nov. 6, 1920) 138–238; "Bootlegging and Murder in Detroit," *The Literary Digest* LXXVIII (Sept. 29, 1923) 48–53; "'Shooting' Detroit Bootleggers with a Camera," *The Literary Digest* LXXIX (Dec. 29, 1923) 34–36; F. L. Smith, "War on the River," *Outlook* (July 24, 1929); Morrow Mayo, "Rum Running on the Detroit River," *The Nation* CXXIX (Sept. 4, 1929) 42; Walter Liggett, "Michigan—Soused and Serene," *Plain Talk* VI (March 1930) 257–73; N. H. Bowen, "Liquor Fights Have Stirred Michigan for Over 75 Years," *Detroit Saturday Night* (December 10, 1921); R. J. McLauchlin, " Ecorse, Thanks to Mr. Volstead, Finds the River a Stream of Gold," *Detroit Saturday Night* (August 20, 1921); A New Detroiter, "Rum Running Typists," *New York Times* (June 6, 1922); James C. Young, "Rum War Forces Mass on the Detroit Front," *New York Times* (June 23, 1929); and Charles Selden, "Our Rum Capital: An Amazing Picture," *New York Times* (May 27, 1928).

Newspapers in Detroit, Port Huron, Sault St. Marie, Toledo, Cleveland, and Columbus as well as Windsor, Toronto, and Kingston, gave extensive coverage to rumrunning, liquor wars, speakeasies and blind pigs, court trials, police matters, and other violations of federal, state, and local liquor laws. See, for example:

"One Hundred Customs Men to Be Fired," *Detroit News* (Dec. 1, 1928); "Flashing Light Signals Guide Smugglers Across River," *Detroit News* (May 2, 1928).

More recently newspapers have run feature articles about Prohibition. See: Barbara Hoover, "The Repeal of an Era," *Detroit News Magazine* (July 17, 1983); Ted Taipalus, "The River and the Rummers," *Detroit News Magazine* (July 17, 1983); "When Booze Was Illegal," *Port Huron Times Herald* (Feb. 5, 1990); and Jill Carson, "Speak Easy Keeps Wolf from Family Door," *Port Huron Times Herald* (Feb. 5, 1990).

For rumrunning on Lake St. Clair see: Mary Karshner, "Blossom Heath," *Muskrat Tales* V (Spring 1988) 10–18; and Cynthia Bieniek, "Rumrunning Days on Lake St. Clair," *Muskrat Tales* 6 (Winter 1993).

The best account of Prohibition in Windsor and the Detroit River is C. H. Gervais, *The Rumrunners: A Prohibition Scrapbook* (Scarborough, Ont.: Firefly Books, 1980).

Also of value is C. H. Gervais, *The Border Police: One Hundred and Twenty–Five Years of Policing in Windsor* (Waterloo, Ont: Penumbra Press, 1992); Neil F. Morrison, *Garden Gateway to Canada* (Windsor, Ont.: Herald Press, 1954) 287–90; Albert Corey, *Canadian Relations Along the Detroit River* (Detroit: Wayne State University Press, 1957); Gerald A. Hallowell, " Prohibition in Ontario," (M.A. Thesis, Carleton University, 1966); and C. W. Hunt, *Booze, Boats and Billions* (Toronto: McClelland and Stewart, 1988).

For Detroit connections relating to rum-running on the Mexican border see Harvey Patton, "Gun Fights Frequent in Whiskey Running on Mexican Border," *Detroit Saturday Night* (May 7, 1921).

Archival Sources

Extensive primary sources are available on all phases of Prohibition on the Michigan–Ontario waterway including U.S. federal, state, and local and Canadian federal, provincial, and local archives. The U.S. National Archives has the files of numerous departments and units that were involved in Prohibition. Of special importance are the record groups relating to the U.S. Coast Guard, the U.S. Treasury Department, the U.S. Food Administration, the Department of Justice, the Bureau of Internal Revenue, the Bureau of Industrial Alcohol, and the National Commission on Law Observance and Enforcement.

The records of the U.S. District Court for the Eastern District of Michigan in the Federal Records Center in Chicago contain information on several thousand court trials. The James Couzens Papers at the Library of Congress are especially valuable. The Michigan State Archives also has extensive relevant material. See, for example, the record groups of the Michigan Attorney General, the Department of State Police, and the State Food and Drug Commission. The official files of Governors Alex Groesbeck and Fred Green also have relevant material on Prohibition.

The Bentley Library of the University of Michigan has several key collections relating to the history of the temperance movement as well as Prohibition. The files of Arthur J. Tuttle, U.S. District Court Judge, have extensive material on Prohibition, including boxes of scrapbooks with clippings on Volstead Act violations. Also valuable are the collections of Governor William Comstock, Henry B. Joy, Pliny Marsh, William J. Martin, and Howard Russell. For additional information see Randall C. Jimerson, Francis X. Blouin, and Charles Isetts, *Guide to the Microfilm Edition of Temperance and Prohibition Papers* (Ann

Arbor: University of Michigan, 1977).

The Burton Historical Collections of the Detroit Public Library holds extensive material in Detroit's role in Prohibition, including the papers of the mayors, Corporation Council, and Detroit Police Department. The collection of Congressman Robert Clancy, an outspoken critic of Prohibition, is also valuable. The archives of Detroit area communities are also important, especially the court and police files. See, for example, the records of the Grosse Pointe Park Police for the period from 1920 to 1931.

INDEX

TITLES IN THE
GREAT LAKES BOOKS SERIES

An Afternoon in Waterloo Park, by Gerald Dumas, 1988 (reprint)

Contemporary Michigan Poetry: Poems from the Third Coast, edited by Michael Delp, Conrad Hilberry, and Herbert Scott, 1988

Over the Graves of Horses, by Michael Delp, 1988

Wolf in Sheep's Clothing: The Search for a Child Killer, by Tommy McIntyre, 1988

Copper-Toed Boots, by Marguerite de Angeli, 1989 (reprint)

Detroit Images: Photographs of the Renaissance City, edited by John J. Bukowczyk and Douglas Aikenhead, with Peter Slavcheff, 1989

Hangdog Reef: Poems Sailing the Great Lakes, by Stephen Tudor, 1989

Detroit: City of Race and Class Violence, revised edition, by B. J. Widick, 1989

Deep Woods Frontier: A History of Logging in Northern Michigan, by Theodore J. Karamanski, 1989

Orvie, The Dictator of Dearborn, by David L. Good, 1989

Seasons of Grace: A History of the Catholic Archdiocese of Detroit, by Leslie Woodcock Tentler, 1990

The Pottery of John Foster: Form and Meaning, by Gordon and Elizabeth Orear, 1990

The Diary of Bishop Frederic Baraga: First Bishop of Marquette, Michigan, edited by Regis M. Walling and Rev. N. Daniel Rupp, 1990

Walnut Pickles and Watermelon Cake: A Century of Michigan Cooking, by Larry B. Massie and Priscilla Massie, 1990

The Making of Michigan, 1820–1860: A Pioneer Anthology, edited by Justin L. Kestenbaum, 1990

America's Favorite Homes: A Guide to Popular Early Twentieth-Century Homes, by Robert Schweitzer and Michael W. R. Davis, 1990

Beyond the Model T: The Other Ventures of Henry Ford, by Ford R. Bryan, 1990

Life after the Line, by Josie Kearns, 1990

Michigan Lumbertowns: Lumbermen and Laborers in Saginaw, Bay City, and Muskegon, 1870–1905, by Jeremy W. Kilar, 1990

Detroit Kids Catalog: The Hometown Tourist, by Ellyce Field, 1990

Waiting for the News, by Leo Litwak, 1990 (reprint)

Detroit Perspectives, edited by Wilma Wood Henrickson, 1991

Life on the Great Lakes: A Wheelsman's Story, by Fred W. Dutton, edited by William Donohue Ellis, 1991

Copper Country Journal: The Diary of Schoolmaster Henry Hobart, 1863–1864, by Henry Hobart, edited by Philip P. Mason, 1991

John Jacob Astor: Business and Finance in the Early Republic, by John Denis Haeger, 1991

Survival and Regeneration: Detroit's American Indian Community, by Edmund J. Danziger, Jr., 1991

Steamboats and Sailors of the Great Lakes, by Mark L. Thompson, 1991

Cobb Would Have Caught It: The Golden Years of Baseball in Detroit, by Richard Bak, 1991

Michigan in Literature, by Clarence Andrews, 1992

Under the Influence of Water: Poems, Essays, and Stories, by Michael Delp, 1992

The Country Kitchen, by Della T. Lutes, 1992 (reprint)

The Making of a Mining District: Keweenaw Native Copper 1500–1870, by David J. Krause, 1992

Kids Catalog of Michigan Adventures, by Ellyce Field, 1993

Henry's Lieutenants, by Ford R. Bryan, 1993

Historic Highway Bridges of Michigan, by Charles K. Hyde, 1993

Lake Erie and Lake St. Clair Handbook, by Stanley J. Bolsenga and Charles E. Herndendorf, 1993

Queen of the Lakes, by Mark Thompson, 1994

Iron Fleet: The Great Lakes in World War II, by George J. Joachim, 1994

Turkey Stearnes and the Detroit Stars: The Negro Leagues in Detroit, 1919–1933, by Richard Bak, 1994

Pontiac and the Indian Uprising, by Howard H. Peckham, 1994 (reprint)

Charting the Inland Seas: A History of the U.S. Lake Survey, by Arthur M. Woodford, 1994 (reprint)

Ojibwa Narratives of Charles and Charlotte Kawbawgam and Jacques LePique, 1893–1895. Recorded with Notes by Homer H. Kidder, edited by Arthur P. Bourgeois, 1994, co–published with the Marquette County Historical Society

Strangers and Sojourners: A History of Michigan's Keweenaw Peninsula, by Arthur W. Thurner, 1994

Win Some, Lose Some: G. Mennen Williams and the New Democrats, by Helen Washburn Berthelot, 1995

Sarkis, by Gordon and Elizabeth Orear, 1995

The Northern Lights: Lighthouses of the Upper Great Lakes, by Charles K. Hyde, 1995 (reprint)

Kids Catalog of Michigan Adventures, second edition, by Ellyce Field, 1995

Rumrunning and the Roaring Twenties: Prohibition on the Michigan–Ontario Waterway, by Philip P. Mason, 1995